OTHER BOOKS
BY THE AUTHOR:

From Time to Time

The Dreamer's Manifesto

The Money Game

STEPPING BEYOND INTENTION

DANIEL MANGENA

Stepping Beyond Intention is published by Phoenex Publishing, UK

ISBN: 978-1-9999571-1-7 paperback
ISBN: 978-1-9999571-5-5 ebook

www.DreamWithDan.com

First Edition 2019.
Second Edition 2021.

TABLE OF CONTENTS

Preface vii

Introduction 1

The Choice Machine 7

    The Beyond Intention Flow Funnel 12

    Owning Where You Are 17

    You Are the Common Denominator 20

    Intentions 21

    The Intention-Setting Process 26

    The Path of Least Resistance 32

    What is Your Why? 35

Beyond Intention: Paradigm in Action 40

    Applying Beyond Intention to Your Life 42

Beyond Intention Step One: Accept 46

    Time for Another exercise. 50

    Stepping into Your Power 52

Beyond Intention Step Two: Clear 57

    Reframing and Re-educating 62

    Your Personal Clearing Toolkit. 69

    "If you're doing everything right, then
       nothing is going wrong." 72

Recap: Tying It All Together So You Can Move
    into Your Future 74

Beyond Intention Step Three: Gratitude 77

    The Intersection of Gratitude and
       Quantum Physics 79

    Gratitude as a Way of Life 84

    Changing Your Programs for the Long Term . . 91

Beyond Intention Step Four: Listen. 94

    Patience, Shifts, and Outcomes 98

    The Receiving Mode: Holding the Frequency
       with Beyond Intention 101

    Celebrations... and Why We Celebrate 107

    Stacking and Staying Present to Your Creation . 111

    Dreaming with Your Eyes Open 118

Closing Thoughts. 121

What Comes Next? 123

    Case Studies & Testimonials. 127

    Who is Daniel Mangena? 143

    Clearing Tools Encyclopedia 145

PREFACE

It was cold—I mean really cold. Hand warmers inside the gloves activated, thermal underwear on, hat, scarf, multiple layers, and yet my fingers and toes were still numb. While walking meditations take about an hour and twenty minutes, they really feel like a blur of bliss when you lose yourself in them.

It was February in Santa Fe, New Mexico, and the meditation retreat I was attending had ended the day prior. To date, it had been my most challenging one. Not only had I *not* dropped into the meditations as deeply as I had been hoping to, but I had also placed excess pressure on myself to get something meaningful, life-altering, or mystical out of it.

All the same, I had spent seven days in over thirty hours of deep meditation, and as is still customary for me, I did a final walking meditation before heading home on the day after the event. As dawn gave way to morning, the rising sun lent some heat to warm me.

With the event now over, and having fallen short of my mind's busy intended outcomes, I was in a relaxed state of surrender. This made it much easier to finally have no expectations, which was precisely why I was floored by what awaited me.

And so, when the walking meditation came to an end, there it was, that moment of awareness I had been seeking the entire event.

In an instant, I was transported back through time, witnessing how everything I had experienced and been through in my life had led me to this present moment where I was able—for the very first time—to truly see what it meant to be grateful. Sure, I'd had surface gratitude for parts of my journey, as the easy stuff is easy stuff, as they say.

> *'It was easy to love God in all that was beautiful. The lessons of deeper k nowledge, though, instructed me to embrace God in all things.'*
>
> **— Saint Francis of Assisi**

So there I was, humbled by more joy than I knew what to do with. In an instant, every ounce of shame and pain that had once enslaved me was transmuted into the light of gratitude; the vision of my future and the path toward it had been lit for me.

An inner voice and inner knowing told me that my life would never be the same. I no longer had a choice to ignore the calling, one which I had been averting and running from for years.

INTRODUCTION

> *'Scientia potentia est - Knowledge itself is power'*
>
> **— Sir Francis Bacon**

They say that knowledge has nothing to do with our ability to remember, but rather, to truly *know* something is to be able to apply its usage in practical terms.

I am here to share with you the knowledge I have learned about the power of intention, as well as the steps you can take in your daily life to wield it as a force for creation.

To begin, I ought to explain that this is not the book I originally wanted to share with you. After eleven years and at least five very different drafts, I finally settled on the vision of what this book would be. In doing so, I prepared myself to lay my soul bare before you, all the while taking you on a journey with the many twists and turns that brought Beyond Intention to the world.

But what I just didn't realize at the time was that I wasn't ready.

The level of vulnerability I would need to share that much of myself with the world was not something I could do—not up until now.

So I have finally committed, and commit to you now, to give you that honest, vulnerable book that will take you from *Vision, Purpose, Faith, Gratitude*—the model that predated *Beyond Intention*—to the failure of that which nearly brought me to the edge of suicide, and ultimately to the moment when Step One of Beyond Intention was born.

That first step is Acceptance.

From there, I will take you to the most up-to-date expression of Alchemic Life Creation, the place to which the name of this paradigm, Beyond Intention, alludes.

To begin, I want to tell you there is no guru who can save you and no answers you can simply pluck from thin air, nor any magical trickery you can call upon. The reason why is that the answers you seek are already within you, and it is from your own depths that these answers must come to you.

You are the miracle, and I am simply a messenger.

The purpose of this book is to show you how to break through the stagnant energy and paralyzed states of being that only hinder your development. These are the angst-inducing places and spaces in your existence where you get the feeling there has to be more to life—and that there's a better way for you to live it—and yet you can't quite figure out what that is or how to get there.

Even if you're armed with all the theoretical knowledge in the world, if you don't know how to apply that knowledge in your daily life, what possible good is it? You need practical steps to not only set your intentions for a better life, but also to give you the tools required to live them.

This book aims to show you how to do that, and I thank you for trusting me to assist in your journey.

At this moment, you are one of approximately 7.8 billion people now living on this planet, a vast proportion of whom are struggling against what they see as impossible odds and against a lifestyle that only seems to work against them—no matter how much energy they invest in it.

By choosing this book, you have decided to stop struggling against the overwhelming inertia of life's drudgery, and in that act, declared that you are prepared to make substantial changes. Think about that for a second.

You being here, you reading this right now, is not a coincidence.

Join me Beyond Intention and open your mind to a paradigm of pure intention made to manifest in your life—deliberately, on command, and each time you set out to do so.

While I'm not a scientist, a mystic, or a sage, I've spent some time in the mystery schools, and for nearly twenty years, learned at the feet of all three. Instead, just like you, I am a student of life, so will not speak outside my areas of knowledge and experience.

Thus, if at some point you think that I should have or could have delved deeper into this or that, know that I feel it's my responsibility to only explore *as far as I know*—since the world is filled with enough people who talk about what they do *not* know—and to point you toward credible and authoritative resources for yet more insight.

Throughout this book, I will endeavor to direct you to those additional resources wherever possible, adding depth and substance to the ideas explored in this introductory journey into my work.

All I ask in return is for your patience where certain leaps are made, and that before rejecting any concepts I have expounded upon in this book, you look a little deeper yourself, seeing where it carries you.

For more information on my work, as well as some free resources to support you on your journey, please visit www.DreamWithDan.com.

For some reminders of how to stay on track with your transformation and evolution, I also encourage you to connect with me on social media where my handle is @dreamerceo.

Yours in abundance,
Dan.

THE CHOICE MACHINE

If you were to take a little time to reflect on who you are in the present moment, you might find that who you call *you*—right here and right now—is a collection of ideas, stories, and memories of so many people, places, and things that have been a part of your journey thus far.

You don't agree?

Well then, consider this.

Briefly close your eyes and envisage your favorite food. Picture it on the plate, the bone or the stick, or however it represents itself.

Now take a mouthful of this culinary delight. Taste it, smell it, feel its texture in your mouth—and engage all your senses in this experience. In your mind's eye, feel each mastication, then swallow it and follow its gentle route down your throat into your stomach. Savour the enjoyment, and when you're ready, open your eyes again.

Well done! You just time traveled.

You see, your consciousness can't be in more than one place at the same time, so the fact you managed to divert your attention and thought to another place and time where you were experiencing your favorite food, indicates your consciousness managed to convey itself to the past or future and succeeded in experiencing that food while your body was still rooted in the present.

This experience now forms a part of who you consider yourself to be and of how your life is.

You had to reflect on the memory of your favorite food and connect to the flavor, sensation, and texture to form the image of your opinion that this dish comprises your favorite food.

Did you realize all of this happened in the past?

Even if you'd had the dish in front of you at this moment, by the time you ingested the food and made the cognitive connection to the emotion making it your favorite, you were still returning to a prior experience—or multiple experiences—of eating it.

You were returning to a memory or memories of the past so you could place the food into your perceptions in the present, and this all goes well beyond food, of course.

Every single aspect of your life which you use to reflect or consider who you are relates to the past. Everything.

I could even say that every thought you consider is based on a past event or action stored in the memory banks of your mind. Therefore, it's fair to say that your state of being is based on the totality of recalling past experiences, creating the basis for your understanding of who you are.

Since that's the case, if you truly want to transform your life, it all comes down to creating an immediate future vision of *who you want to be*—and setting in place steps to accomplish your life goals.

But it's always the memories of past events and occur-rences that form the basis for your self-perception, and so the memories upon which you define all your expe-riences come from somewhere deep within the mind.

Further, the experiences that form these memories— later to be called upon—are the result of your own, individual life journey.

Your own journey will have started at a point in time when—of all the possible paths available—you stepped into a timeline associated with *the trajectory leading to the outcome you experienced*. But selecting that path, too, did not happen by chance. Whether consciously or subconsciously, you made a choice to follow that route.

Whether it's a choice you've made to go left or right, or it's something you regretfully said, or whether it was staying in bed five minutes longer, accepting that date, or indulging in life's many non-essentials, every single one of these choices came about as the result of selecting a path, the outcome of which became an experience. That experience became a memory, forming the basis of your identity and how your self-image came into being.

That means most of the time, who you *are* is a memory of who you *were*. Why? Because as you look back on your experiences, love or admiration for a certain person could stem from a positive experience shared with them. Likewise, people you dislike or choose to avoid could derive from an unpleasant experience aligning to what you know as *dislike.*

Well, true freedom comes in being no longer enslaved to the sways of past memories and reflections that are charged with emotions. This is a big part of the work that's required in Alchemic Life Creation.

When you do the work to gain emotional freedom, you can use tools to effectively change the patterns of who you are right at this very moment. You can achieve this by examining what engendered your journey and experiences—the ones that formed the basis of all the beliefs and visions you hold for yourself.

As an example, when you look back at the love of your life, was there really a monumental point in time that evolved in your decision to meet them? Probably not. Most often, it's more about the very subtle movements that just happened to lead you to the right place at the right time. But every single one of those harkens back to a point in time when either, consciously or subconsciously, the choice was made to walk toward the path that led to the profound experience of love.

You may now find yourself thinking, *ok, but so what*? *Yes, these choices created the outcomes I experience, but how does this add to my life?*

By stepping into the operator's chair of your choice machine, you step into the driver's seat of your life. What is the choice machine? The choice machine is the engine that creates the outcomes that you will experience, through the choices you make in the now.

In this book, you will learn how to choose in the present moment the paths that lead to the outcomes you desire for the future. Essentially, you'll be learning how to direct the energy in your life so that you can have a *deliberate* life, one in which you are the leader, not the led.

In short, deliberate choices lead to a deliberate life. By applying the learning from this book, you will be empowered to live intentionally and step out of the random sway of outcomes that form a life short of the one you truly deserve.

The Beyond Intention Flow Funnel

Since ancient times, sacred texts have referenced the triumvirate of the mind, body, and soul. Today, there exist many variants of the same idea, often referred to as spiritual, mental, and physical, or thoughts, actions, and feelings. Or even heaven, hell, and earth.

I first shared the flow funnel of this model and its relationship to the Beyond Intention paradigm in my Micro-2Millions group coaching program. It was there—in relation to creating financial abundance—that I saw how well this idea could support students in understanding **how** people's intentions show up in the world, as well as what happens behind the curtain when they do not.

It's important to recognize that if ancient wisdom is correct, the power of choice to create an outcome resides in creating an alignment of energy/emotions, with mindset/beliefs, and with actions within the physical environment. Every resistance-free thought in how you feel, what you believe, and what you do shows up for you as an exact science. The outcomes that do *not* appear in your life have become trapped or blocked in one or more of those areas.

As people progress through their lives—ones that include constant obstacles and challenges—the real work is in consistently choosing to be in alignment with intention; therefore, it's integral to have a framework to do so. And as we take our students and clients through any of our coaching workshops, courses, or programs, this is the foundational skill.

While I go into greater detail on the flow funnel in much of my content on YouTube, I also have several podcast episodes dedicated to its deeper understanding. For the purpose of this book, however, I would like to give you a basic understanding, specifically in its relation to the work of Beyond Intention.

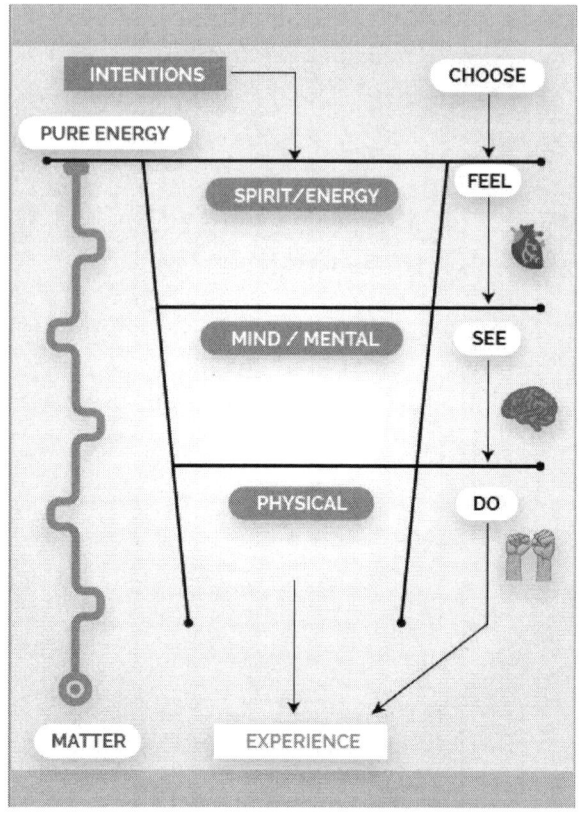

Essentially, there are three environments or levels of density through which thought descends en route to becoming the physical matter you experience with your senses.

They are the:

- *Spirit or Energy Environment*

- *Mental Environment*
- *Physical Environment.*

The Energy Environment is where you connect with spirit and energy. You will generally relate to this environment with your senses and feelings. Therefore, in Beyond Intention, I say that once you have your intention, you must be able to feel it.

So, the Flow Funnel invites you to take your intention through a deliberate journey of:

1. INTENDING: Consciously choose a thought, goal or desire.

2. FEELING: Use your heart to feel the thought/ intention. Connect to how you will feel when you have achieved your intention.

3. BELIEVING: See or mentally rehearse in your mind's eye the possibility of the intention. What you are doing is mentally observing the occurrence or fruition of the intention *before* you experience it.

4. ACTING: Act in accordance with your beliefs with regard to how your intention must come to the experience. This creates alignment with your inner world. You achieve this by acting as if the intention has already manifested. To act as such is to live in a state of positive expectation—it's to have gratitude for the outcome

of the potential. Now you simply need to connect to that intention, as opposed to living in
fear or that it will not come to be, or lacking it.
(More on this later).

Intend, Feel, Believe, Act...then Experience

Again, this is a very quick exploration of the model.
My book *"The Money Game"*, spends time going into
greater deal of detail into these steps, using the manifestation of money as the example.

In other areas of our work, we specifically demonstrate
how to use the Beyond Intention paradigm to remove
the resistance that prevents the experience coming
into fruition. A great place to start is *"Beyond Intention
Foundations"*, a short, practical, simple to follow audio
program that teaches you exactly how to use Beyond
Intention for this purpose.

It is important to remember that although the spiritual,
mental, and physical environments that bring intention
into matter/reality are stacked on each other from a
position of dependence, in actual execution, they are
much more fluid and interconnected.

In truth, just as time is an illusion, or more so—a collective belief agreed upon by the masses—you might
perceive that the journey through the funnel happens
in linear time.

The illustration above is designed to enable a clear overview of the process, which is actually all happening *now*, in the present moment. It all just depends on the level of energy with which the person meets the intention within the present moment.

For a detailed set of directions as to how to use this model to create financial abundance in your life, check out Making The Money Game Work in the free resources section of my website.

Owning Where You Are

He looked angrily at the desk clerk at JFK Airport Terminal 3, bewildered at the words he was hearing.

"I'm sorry, sir, but we just can't help you. There is no record of you on this flight or any other flight. We've checked the flight manifest manually, and your name's just not there."

He was livid. He had set his intention on being in Toronto the following morning with grace and ease. He'd booked and paid for his accommodation, and even had his uber-efficient German travel assistant, Julia, make all the arrangements.

It was 3 a.m. in Germany, so Julia was not awake, yet he called her anyway. Could she have made a mistake? But he was sure it wasn't so; he trusted her so implicitly that she didn't even have to give him booking confirmations.

For the entirety of their time together, he had always just shown up at the airport, with Julia having taken care of the booking. There had never been a problem before.

Bewildered, he begrudgingly canceled his appearance the next morning on the TV show for which he was booked, and made his way back to his apartment. Yet still, none of it made sense. All the planning had been so efficient and detailed; how could it have let him down?

He'd arrived at the airport on time, made sure his baggage didn't weigh too much, and even had his toiletries already sorted out into those clear little plastic bags! But clearly, despite all this meticulous attention to detail, something had gone wrong.

There was one problem, however, which was revealed to him by a conversation the following morning with Julia.

He was at the wrong airport, looking for the wrong plane, at the wrong time.

And yup, that person was me.

Long story short, I had looked at a number of flights and mistakenly shown up for the wrong one. I was supposed to have been at Newark airport to get an 8 p.m. flight on United, not JFK for a 9 p.m. flight on Delta.

As silly as this example may seem, the point is that so often, people travel through life buying plane tickets to the right destination, yet fail miserably in being at the correct airport at the correct time. And the same applies to you.

All of your visualization, all of your energy work, all of your meditation, and all of your actions mean nothing whatsoever if they are not firmly grounded in an honest grasp of where you are in the here and now.

It doesn't matter *why* you are at the wrong airport. You may have been exhausted, or maybe you were so engaged in visualizing where you wanted to be that you forgot where you were. All I know is that when creating new outcomes, you must acknowledge the reality of where you are in the present moment.

This type of honest reflection is not an exercise to beat yourself up or to inflict guilt or shame as to where you currently are in your life's journey. This is an empowering opportunity to embrace the knowledge you have in this moment of truth—that this moment too shall pass. It's a recognition that what will be born of your current and future experiences will come about as a result of the choices you make here and now.

So what does the here and now look like? Are you in a loveless relationship? In a job you dislike? Regretful of past decisions? Whether these situations are a result of conscious or unconscious behaviors and choices, you need to own those decisions and the truth of those decisions as a creation of your own doing. Every seed that led to your current experience was planted by you at some level of consciousness. The beauty of gaining a new awareness in the present moment, however, is that every seed you plant from here on out comes under the domain of your creative, intentional power—if you choose to accept it

The bottom line is, you need to take ownership. Once you do, you can set intentions, and the resistance to the fruition of your intention can be aligned, enabling you to create the outcomes you most desire in your life.

You Are the Common Denominator

If you look back at all the experiences in your life, the only constant is that *you* are at the center of each one.

In every win. In every lesson. In every challenge. *There you are.*

This simple truth came to me at a truly dark time in my life, and it was this recognition that pulled me back from the brink of taking my own life. *I* was the one at the center of every experience I sought to escape. So the reality of things was obvious: if I could change me, then I could change it all.

That moment of insight was the birth of Beyond Intention and the start of my journey toward my true purpose here on earth. It was born of a situation where I had every reason to push blame in 100 different directions, but the joy I have in my life today stems directly from owning this.

As you begin setting intentions, it may serve you to look within and take responsibility for where *you* are. Reject the dangling carrot your mind may use in an attempt to steer you toward allocating blame, which is the way the mind entices you to give away your power to other people, situations, events, and happenings.

The purpose of this book is to start the process of opening you up to your own power—because power is choice.

What do I mean?

I mean the one thing present in every life experience is that you have the choice to remain who you are and where you are or to change who you are and where you are going. It all comes down to your decision, and only you are in control of that.

Intentions

I ran a Google search on the word *intention* and the following were amongst the generated definitions:

- Something that you want and plan to do
- An act or instance of determining mentally upon some action or result

- A thing intended; an aim or plan.

An intention in its purest form is not something you can touch or taste. It originates as a thought—generated from within the mind—the experience of which, once manifested in your physical reality (governed by your beliefs and cognitive perceptions) becomes an experience that you can then measure and engage with your senses.

So an intention is a thought. Moreover, it is a thought deliberately curated for the purpose of bringing about a specific experience or outcome.

Looking back at the flow funnel, I could say then that because people are always thinking, they are always populating their funnels with instructions. This is clearly true because people are always experiencing something.

Intentions may be viewed as a way of introducing conscious guidance to what otherwise—according to renowned cellular biologist Dr. Bruce Lipton—is a subconscious process for as much as 95% of a person's day.

As an example, five-year-old Philip snuck downstairs in the act of defiance. His older sister Marie loved horror movies and planned to enjoy the movie *IT*. She sent Philip to bed early with the warning that the movie would likely give him nightmares. Feeling defiant and not wanting to go to bed early, with the skill of a ninja, he crept out of his bed and slipped downstairs.

Breathing in his victory, as he peered through the cracks of the door, he chanced upon a bloody scene where a character carried out gruesome acts of violence. At that moment, he made the cognitive connection that clowns were monsters, and this created fear and anxiety in his body.

With this cognitive connection, at that moment, Philip formed a belief that clowns were monsters. And until this belief became undone, every time he saw a clown, his body would respond to the feelings of fear and anxiety that the memory engendered. In turn, this experience generated an unconscious program.

Although this is a seemingly benign example, for many people, these types of experiences can be crippling. Why? Because of the unique features of the individual, an experience may be so jarring it traps energy in the body. We are all very different, and each of us has our own experiences drawn from the various inputs and interactions in our lives. Thus, what is benign to one person can be quite heart wrenching for another.

Many fears are rational, on the other hand. Fire can kill, and heights, if not respected, can be our end, as can venomous snakes and spiders.

As the author and creator of your life, and based on the library of physical, mental, and emotional evidence stored in the mind on a moment-moment basis, to be intentional is to be able to bring choice into an experience.

It means being capable and conscious of deciding whether to react to a particular situation that otherwise may have been directed and been at the will of your subconscious mind, rather than your awareness in the present moment.

A few years ago, when I skydived over the Nevada desert, I witnessed this firsthand. There were people in my group whose fear of heights stopped them from making the jump. While my rational fear was present, I was open to pushing the limits of my fear so I could step into—and expand into—a new experience.

Just as the sight of a clown can create an *undesirably unconscious* program, being intentional empowers you to plant the seeds of a *desirably conscious* program. As you move deeper into the Beyond Intention paradigm, you will learn more about how to do this, as well as how to break through stuck states and trapped energy that blocks your flow funnel.

Being able to be conscious and deliberate in your intentions allows the mind to open to new evidence, updating the belief system that acts as a filter for what you experience. As evidence deliberately brought in creates space for your belief system to expand, you are also creating the potential for new possibilities in your life.

Without this conscious disruption, the mind will continue to run on old programs, playing out the same patterns, and getting the same results. As an example regarding the fear of heights, fear should no longer hold you back from experiencing the beauty of a mountaintop or the exhilaration of a skydive.

By setting intentions, you are using deliberate thought to direct the creation process, a process that carries the thought from pure energy all the way through the flow funnel into the physical matter—as well as the associated outputs of feeling, body memory, and either disrupted or reinforced beliefs.

Beyond Intention, as you will see, is a dual process, the first of which is learning to hack the system in the short term to create outcomes in the present moment.

The second part of the process is deliberately disrupting and resetting the unconscious programs in which you operate as much as 95% of the time. When you successfully reset the system, the body no longer resists your intentions. Instead, it is open to infinite possibility, therefore allowing the purpose that you plug into your funnel.

The Intention-Setting Process

'It is not enough that you should have a wish to travel, see things, live more, etc. Everybody has those desires also. If you were going to send a wireless message to a friend, you would not send the letters of the alphabet in their order, and let him construct the message for himself; nor would you take words at random from the dictionary. You would send a coherent sentence; one which meant something. When you try to impress your wants upon Substance, remember that it must be done by a coherent statement; you must know what you want, and be definite. You can never get rich, or start the creative power into action, by sending out unformed longings and vague desires.'

The above quote is from *The Science of Getting Rich*, by Wallace D Wattles, one of the five books by which I live. Up until now, this brief discourse on intentions has very much been about clearing the path of resistance from your life, a path that has become engrained due to the past experiences that hold you back.

Wattles' work is very much about being deliberate in the pursuit of wealth and financial abundance. He states that it is necessary to be better equipped to fully experience life through the choice that wealth (as energy and medium of exchange) affords. In other words, having the expanded opportunity that money gives you, you can have a fuller life.

Wattles clarifies that to stake a claim in the creative process, your thoughts must be more than a rough outline of an idea or half-hearted wish. They must be a clear direction and a firm impression of what you choose to experience.

You will now look at the Beyond Intention process of setting intentions. This process is the direct result of more than a decade of living, experiencing, exploring, examining, and learning about the science of using deliberate thought to create specific experiences. It includes setting—and most importantly—*living* the result of your intentions.

To begin, the very first thing I want you to think about is also the most critical question...*Where am I now?*

Many times, people go down the road of intention without realizing that the most crucial aspect to consider is where they currently are in their lives. To go forward and achieve their intentions, however, they need to honor everything about where they are right now; their shadows, strengths, and weaknesses, where they have space for expansion, where they desire to change, and where they desire to grow.

Thus, honoring ourselves and our life's journey up until this point is what enables us to create the right roadmap to deliver us along the route to the chosen destination; in turn, this leads to the most effective techniques, strategies, and practices to achieve the desired outcomes.

So—you guessed it—the very first thing I want *you* to do is take a candid look at where you are in this present moment.

The next step is to begin the process of microshifting into an obvious picture of what you want. What is a microshift, you ask? A microshift is a set of small steps, taken consistently, toward the direction of a chosen outcome. In this book, you will gently move one step at a time toward a clearer picture of what you want your intention to be. This reduces the pressure you place upon yourself in the process of creating an out-come, while exponentially increasing your likelihood to succeed.

Over at www.dreamwithdan.com, we are all about working against the backdrop of microshifting through a series of 'minimum deliverables', the very small-est things that we can achieve without resistance or failure. We ask ourselves, *What step, no matter how seemingly insignificant, can I make now in the direction of my intention?*

Microshifting means piecing these steps together in a consistent way.

So, the first thing you'll also do once you know and have accepted where you are, defines the intention or outcome you want to have.

What is the result physically made up of? How will you get there? What will all of your senses take in when you're at the final destination?

Let's break it down into five manageable steps.

Step One: Where are you now? Own where you are in all of your textures, contrasts, ugliness, beauty, and glory. No matter where you are, know that you always have the power to go somewhere else.

Step Two: What does my intention include? What physically or tangibly makes up the form of that outcome?

Step Three: How does it feel?

Step Four: Moving toward your intention.

Step Five: Locking in your *why*.

The thing about intention is that people don't often enter into the process of intention or creating an outcome for the destination itself. Instead, there's something that they experience inside of them when they achieve the goal they aimed for, a payoff at the end of the road. That payoff is something everyone wants to feel.

As an example, if I want a big house, most likely, I don't want a big house just for the sake of having one. I probably want to experience what space will feel like when it's filled with the love and warmth of the people I care about. I want to feel the joy of having friends and family over for celebrations and holidays. So, I don't want it for the house itself—I want it for the payoff of the feelings that it facilitates.

If I'm looking for a relationship, it's not the relationship per se that I want. I desire the feeling of being loved and giving love, of being nurtured, respected, cared for, and connected within the construct of the relationship.

People don't often want money for money's sake either. They want the security, the comfort, the freedom, the feeling of being unlimited, and ultimately, the joy that comes from the freedom of choice. Money is just a symbol of all of that.

So what I want you to do now is take time to work out how it will feel when your intention is a part of your living experience. If you are stuck, then for the purpose of going through these steps and successfully following this formula, start again—and this time pick something nice and easy to practice these principles with.

In terms of immediate needs, practice creating something not too emotionally charged. Once you have your desired creation locked down, apply it at any time to any intention you want to create in your life. But as I said, for now, start nice and light, and describe the emotions you will feel when your creation comes to fruition.

Even if it's a shadow, such as wanting people to know that you can afford that fancy car or fancy watch, get really honest about what it feels like. Remember this is just an exercise.

Now it's time to get practical. All the intentions in the world are useless if you don't do the work of creating alignment with the intention. This is the process by which your purpose shows up in your life.

My slogan *Dream With Your Eyes Open*, and my book, *The Dreamer's Manifesto*, which breaks down how to live in alignment with this ideal, very much reduces to the following what is required to bring your intention to fruition.

Later on, I will also be sharing how you can use my Beyond Intention paradigm with grace and ease to employ the choice machine effectively.

In the context of your intention, executing upon a purpose is about the follow-up steps required as you walk the road toward intention. This may or may not be a direct action in pursuit of the outcome, but I can tell you there is no cookie-cutter approach.

As a result, there are some real-life limitations in how much I can guide you with these few words, so I invite you to arrange a free no-obligation call to assess how you can make the information in this book more actionable and applicable in your life.

Do that by heading over to <u>www.dreamwithdan.com/dive</u> now.

The Path of Least Resistance

So now I want to ask you: What is the minimum deliverable—the most straightforward path of least resistance—that you can execute upon right now, without fail, in this very moment toward your intention?

Where do you see the least resistance? Where can you take a baby step in the direction of creating space in your life to feel the feelings associated with your intended outcome?

From there, ask yourself:

What can I do in 24 hours? What can I do in 7, 30, 60, and 90 days?

Of course, you don't have to wait the entire 30, 60, or 90 days to take this baby step. The length of time does not speak to the grandiosity of the task. It's about creating space for the least resistance, facilitating taking those baby steps.

While you could get all of these items done today, the important thing is setting the bar super low—so low that there is no way you can fail! Minimum deliverables are all about creating a lack of resistance, allowing ease and flow in the direction of the intended outcome. This enables you to build a series of successes that represent to the mind evidence you are truly capable of accomplishing the tasks you set out to accomplish.

Just remember the mind doesn't lie to itself, so when there is a series of evidence contrary to the ideas you've been holding onto for your dear life, all of a sudden you actually have the possibility of moving into new belief systems that support more change. The mind is not your enemy—it just works on the basis of what it has been given as a blueprint.

Therefore, keep the bar low so that the resistance is lower. This makes you more likely to succeed, and therefore to build up a pattern of success. Once you begin seeing these wins, they will create a beautiful momentum where you'll begin manifesting your intended outcome, and this will help you follow through with the creation of future intentions.

Also, keep in mind as you look at this step in the process, that intentions don't come just because you act. Your action plan, therefore, should consider all the three stages of alignment—mind, body, spirit, etc., of which I spoke earlier.

Achieving these wins may require shifting your energy. Maybe you need to alter your mindset to shake loose resistance. Perhaps it's as simple of an intention as a client of mine once had—to get the ball rolling on his business plan by merely creating the Word document on his computer.

All three of these areas must be in alignment to create an outcome, and two-thirds of that formula is an inside job.

We all know those people who read every self-help book under the sun and yet they're still miserable. They meditate or pray for hours on end, yet still fall short of their intended outcomes. They work on themselves every God-given hour they have, yet they still don't feel any lighter for it.

The successful ones are those who get the three aspects of their being in alignment. What I want you to do now is take that intention as a starting point— take how receiving the outcome would feel so you can create that definite pattern of feeling. Then ask yourself, *what can I do to bring those feelings into my life immediately? What can I do in the next 24 hours, 7 days, 30 days, and 90 days?* Make them achievable goals, so there's no room for failure.

This whole process is ALL about minimum deliverables and microshifts. So go ahead, take a pause here, and start creating that roadmap for the next 24 hours, as well as for the next 7, 30, 60, and 90 days. Ready? Begin...

What is Your Why?

The last thing I want to quickly talk to you about in relation to intention is Step Five: *What is your Why? Why do you want what you're creating*?

So often, people believe they want something, but it's frequently the influence of other people, places, and things that have given them the notion of what they think they want.

Maybe everyone else has one of those things, so you feel you need one too? Perhaps you are seeking validation or a boost in self-esteem? Maybe you have been brought up to think this is the way it's supposed to be done?

When you are not the true originator of the desire, what often happens is that alignment becomes more of a challenge. It may be that a temporary alignment is created, but this will tend to fall away, and as a result, you'll either get no real joy from creating the outcome or you'll un-create it through self-sabotage.

The clients I have worked with who hit the brick wall of a mid-life crisis sometimes fall into this category. They work their entire adult life to be the perfect picture of someone else's design, but when the truth of that superficial design becomes real at a soul level, the fall-out can go any one of many ways. In extreme cases, it can go all the way to the darkness of depression, addiction, and in some cases, even suicide.

So, I am sure you will now see that lasting creation must have total alignment, and that success is highly unlikely if you are not the originator of the desire.

There's also another favorable consideration, and that is this: When the going gets tough, as it often does, how are you going to have the gusto, the gumption, or the drive and motivation to really do what you need to do?

How are you going to work on getting the energy and to really work on the internal environment to hold that mindset together? What are you going to draw upon to make those tough calls and hard choices? The leverage of your *why* is a brilliant way to stack the cards in your favor.

Another great tool that we use in Beyond Intention is a concept we refer to as 'Cleaning Your Intention'. Cleaning your Intention, which you will learn about shortly, operates on a number of levels, extending beyond the question of your 'why' and all the way to the spirit of the intention.

I was once challenged as to how we can 'try to be God' in demanding what we want to create. The challenger's view was that man makes plans, and God decides. I called his attention to Proverbs 29:18: 'Where there is no vision, the people perish.'

This person was quite determined to denounce their role in the creative process. I then asked them why they bothered to pray for things, and then even went so far as to point out that in the Bible, Jesus invites others to ask of the Father—in fact, he even instructs them to do so in his name.

What I am driving at here is that sometimes, preconceived notions and ideas have a stake not only in someone's *why*, but also in their *what*. Limited beliefs tend to reach into the realm of filtering out the experiences that are possible. For instance, if you think what you are trying to create is out of alignment with your beliefs—or out of alignment with what you think you are permitted to have or to be—then you are doomed from the get-go.

In our workshops and coaching programs, we do a lot of work on undoing our own resistance to this dreaming process, especially in phase two of our Ideal Life

Blueprint. This is where we identify our stories, stuck states, and energy traps. Then we use the power of microshifting to move through them. We also work in a way that continues honoring our beliefs as they grow, ensuring that there is space for expansion without creating more resistance. As such, we can also empower *you* to push to your very edge without pushing your buttons.

So what I'd like you to do now is *clean your intention* by finding stillness and silence. Then ask yourself these questions:

- Do I really want this?
- Am I really the one asking for this, or is it other people, places, and things to whom I've given my power?
- Is this intention in alignment with my existing beliefs?
- When I'm sitting in my power and owning this, including any shadows, what is my *why?*

You may have more questions, but the trick is not to lose your own self in these questions. Find a method of connecting to the silence that works for you—or book a free consultation with someone on my team to assist you—and take the time to tape, video, or journal the responses in an honest way.

Only use this model for something that you **genuinely** want, because if you follow these steps, then you WILL get it!

Once you take an intention through this process—taking it into the silence, owning where you are, looking at how the outcomes feel, and then sitting with the feelings of that clear picture—you'll be able to begin creating a roadmap, and then it's going to be a hell of a lot easier to get there.

As the author and creator of what you want to bring into your life, the true ownership of the intention must be the real ownership of your power.

BEYOND INTENTION: PARADIGM IN ACTION

For those of you connecting with my work for the first time, the phrase 'Beyond Intention' may seem strange. The name refers to a four-step process that I created over a decade ago to empower you to take back control of your choice machine. The choice machine is the mechanism enabling you to begin making empowered choices, ones that move you in a consciously chosen direction, as opposed to the same old unconscious patterns of the past that produced no results.

Beyond Intention is designed to reprogram the mind's operating system, so you'll no longer need to keep interjecting the conscious mind to override unconscious programs. When successful, this process will start working in unison for your highest and greatest good.

Over the years, the applications of Beyond Intention have become more specific and really taken shape to work in directing this power to choose in a number of ways.

To name a couple of examples, in our workshops, programs, and online classes, our Ideal Life Blueprint has proven to be most effective in designing and executing an abundant, purpose-driven life that our students love and desire. Beyond Intention has also been effective in transforming entrepreneurs and value creators into six- and seven-figure abundance machines through the framework of our Purpose-Driven Peak Performance tools.

With regard to best applying the Beyond Intention paradigm in your life, if you enjoy online learning, I highly recommend taking our Create Your Ideal Life online program, serving as a bridge between the basic Introduction of Beyond Intention and its various applications.

Also check out the Beyond Intention Basics online program for a more in-depth exploration of the four steps of Beyond Intention offered in this book.

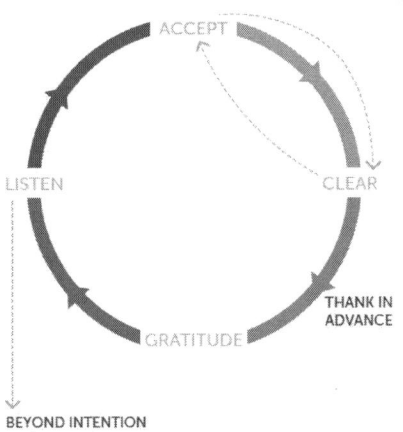

As you can see from the diagram above, there are four steps in the Beyond Intention paradigm:

1. **Accept.** Own that you are the author and creator of your life. Everything that has shown up is yours, and all that is going to show up will be yours as well.

2. **Clear**. You can only create in the now. Discover and apply the tools that bring you back to the Now and cut the ties to the energy traps of the past.

3. **Gratitude**. Reality wraps around how you feel. Call in the feelings of what you want to create, acknowledging everything already existing as a potential outcome and that you can connect to that outcome by feeling grateful for it before it is made manifest.

4. **Listen**. Hold the frequency. Honor that there may be a time lag between intention and experience. During that time, remain aware of where you are in relation to your purpose so that you can make adjustments to stay on course.

Applying Beyond Intention to Your Life

In this section, we're going to teach you some of the basics of the paradigm, as well as give you some examples of how to apply it in your life. You're going to need a pen and paper or whatever device you use to take notes because you'll document your journey throughout this book section.

Once you are done with this book, I really suggest getting yourself a copy of our Dreamer Journal over at www.dreamwithdan.com. The journal is specifically designed to support you on your Beyond Intention journey.

As this is an integral part of the process, I implore you to make time for these steps. At least while you work on this, I ask that you step away from other draining mental activities that pull you out of the present moment and divert your energy from the task at hand. That means no TV. Listening to relaxing music is fine, but not your favorite song. This is no time to dance, time to grow.

There will be exercises in each section, and I'll also be giving you homework. If you like to work with an accountability partner, go ahead and get one. If you don't know what I'm talking about, just head over to www.happiercast.com and see which of the four tendencies you fall into.

You see, this is a very, very important step in rebuilding the programs that have been running your life so far. So, I also invite you to look at www.16personalities.com for more resources to help you invest in yourself and your future.

If you are to evolve into a new state of being, you need to know what you're evolving from.

This helps you to identify which parts of yourself you want to improve, as well as potential pitfalls and challenges along the way.

As you take this journey, I'd really like you to bring your *A-game* so that by the end of this program, you'll see immense growth in at least one area. This isn't about complete and total evolution but more about setting the foundation to evolve on your own terms.

For this program, I'd really love you to focus on just one life area. It could be health, relationships, getting over the past, and so on. It could be a particular stuck state of being or a thought loop you experience. It could be moving into a new job. It doesn't really matter what it is. What's important is that you have one intention to execute as you move into Beyond Intention.

Remember that it's *nobody else's responsibility but yours* to claim this new life. No one else but you holds this power to change—nobody else has the ability to create this new life for you.

You can make all the excuses in the world as to why you won't change, but at the end of the day, it all comes down to you, which is why you're reading this in the first place.

And so the first thing I'd like you to do is write down the reason why you're engaged in this program. Again, this is just for you, so speak honestly to yourself.

Now, I want you to honestly identify at least one thing you feel will be the cause of you not achieving the objective you've set for yourself. If you're here just because you're curious, then write down why you're only sitting on the sidelines and not taking part. Even if the reason is that you're not sure this is something you want to commit to right now, write it down.

The next thing you'll do is write down the first draft of your very own intention based on this objective. However, note that the intention you start with is not as important as having *something* tangible with which to work. As you move through the Beyond Intention paradigm, you may even find that your intention will change, and that's perfectly fine.

I just want you to write something down—to make a commitment in writing to the outcome, the INTEN-TION, toward which you're working.

BEYOND INTENTION
STEP ONE: ACCEPT

Common Denominator Theory forms the basis of the Beyond Intention paradigm.

This theory essentially states that if you want a definitive change, then within yourself is the very best place to start. True strength comes from accepting your power to effect real change in your life via the choices you make, as well as accepting responsibility for the outcomes.

In our coaching programs, we work side by side with clients, making it more feasible to spread the training into other areas of their lives. But for the purpose of this book, we are going to be working specifically to align your intention to each step of the Beyond Intention paradigm. This will give you a solid basis for you to practice working within the paradigm, while applying the principles to get your own real-life results.

As I said, as you work through the process and your learning grows, you will likely be tweaking your intention, but for now, consider that all we have discussed is in relation to the intention you created at the start. Do start making connections with other areas of your life, however, since this will all greatly benefit you—and as more intentions you want to work with pop up, record them. But for now, do steadfastly stick with the one you started, so you can take it all the way through.

So the first exercise is this:

Identify at least one area in your life right now where you blame someone for something you have previously experienced, or even continue to experience. This can be absolutely anything.

Maybe someone makes you late for work all the time, or you hate your job because of your boss. It could be something as profound as you having intimacy issues or that your relationships never work because of the influence of your parents. What it is doesn't honestly matter. What's important is that you start forming these thought processes and building these neural pathways in relation to the process of the Beyond Intention paradigm. So go ahead, make a note of at least one area of your life that you can identify *right now* where you have consistently blamed someone else for something that happens in your life.

Again, one of the key tenets of this step of Beyond Intention is something called Common Denominator Theory.

So whenever you get stuck with a question of responsibility in relation to this intention, I don't want you to go back to default. At the very least, I'd like you to revert to this one point, *that you are at the center of your life's experience.* Does that make sense to you? The bottom line is that in each such occurrence, there is one pivotal factor carrying through every happening, every single time—*and that is you.* You are present in each one, thus you're the common denominator, and logically it's impossible to deny the truth and reality of it.

So, let me say it again!

You are the common denominator of everything that has shown up in your life.

You are the only common thread between every single one of your experiences—all of your relationships, all of the challenges, all of your fears, all of your wins, all of your losses, and every single fight you've had with every single person in your life.

It's important to remember also, however, that every single success you've enjoyed, no matter who you pass off the responsibility to, is equally yours to celebrate. You cannot accept the failures without the triumphs, nor the triumphs without the failures. Accepting you are the common denominator means you're freeing yourself to steer your own path in future.

Now, no longer are you someone else's victim! You manage your own life, the captain of your own ship, to steer it whichever way you desire. Even if—let's say—there is someone else wielding considerable influence over you in some way, you are the one who makes that choice. Say yes to it or say no to it—just steer your ship, recognizing yourself as that common denominator and taking a stand to steer your ship off those precarious and treacherous rocks in future.

Only you can do it. Only you are present in every scenario, for good or ill. Only you are the common denominator.

In one Beyond Intention workshop, we had a woman who on several occasions, had experienced a spontaneous remission from two serious illnesses. Surprisingly, she hadn't acknowledged that the common denominator in both of those instances was her. With tears in her eyes, she was empowered to claim, "I did it", and to own that it was the magic within her that created her healing.

You may think that is easy to say, and even somewhat glib, but it's true. You only have to look around you to find two people with a similar ailment who approach it in very disparate ways—one with complete negativity, saying, "I will never get a better life while I have this," and another facing it and confronting it head on. The latter person doesn't take no for an answer. He or she says in the face of adversity, "Fine, I'm stuck with you for now but you won't beat me. You picked the wrong person to mess with!"

So, which of those two people are you? And are you an accepter of the Common Denominator Theory or are you going to stay in denial?

Time for Another Exercise...

I'd like you to go back to the area of your life you iden-tified in the last exercise—where you acknowledged placing the blame on someone else—and I'd like you to write down at least one way in which you contributed to the outcome to which you were referring.

Let's say, for example, it was a case of always being late for work. Write down one way in which you contributed to the outcome. Maybe you should have gotten up or left the house earlier. Maybe you should have said no to those extra glasses of wine last night that made you oversleep, or perhaps you should have refused to take someone else's kid to school again this morning. Ouch, harsh, isn't it? Sometimes so, but it's true.

Which one of you is to blame if the neighbor asked you to take little Jonny to school and you said yes? Who held the cards there? You did. You see where I'm headed with this. So write down that thing, that one way in which you contributed to the outcome that ended up being bad for you.

What's important is that you find the one thing, no matter how trivial, and recognize the way in which you contributed to it. Don't get caught up in self-admonishment or horror—just say *it is what it is,* write it down, and learn from it.

Now, unfortunately, here's where even I concede that you do all have quite a legitimate complaint, which is that as much as 70% of the subconscious programs that you run on a day-to-day basis were at some point given to you by your environments. A large chunk of those programs happened between the ages of two and seven when generally speaking, you didn't really have the mental faculties for filtering what was being taught to you.

Then there are also community and culture, which imprinted ideas on you as you were growing up.

As an example, if you grew up in an area not culturally diverse, you may hold certain opinions based on a lack of knowledge of other cultures—opinions that might then be reinforced by popular culture, the media, and other forms of propaganda.

Through the power of choice and the beauty of awareness, however, here's where you're at right now:

the reality of the here and now is that you don't have to remain a slave to those subconscious programs you've always run on. Instead, you have the opportunity to move in a new and more positive direction and forge an original path based on new thinking.

Thus, again you are the one with the choice here. You can either accept what was meted out to you and say, well, *I was brought up that way and I am who I am,* or you can recognize how those views just don't serve you and make a step toward change.

It's a fact that subconscious programs come to us all from inputs. By changing the inputs, you can, therefore, shift the program here in Beyond Intention. As a general principle, what you're doing is shifting the overall program. Therefore, from that new state of being, you have the opportunity to make new choices, and those new choices create new experiences, and those new experiences form an empowered and joyful new life for you.

The bottom line is, you and you alone are in the driver's seat of your life, and not the passenger seat. So with that in mind, I'd like you to record and reflect on at least one area of your life where you feel some resistance to this statement.

Stepping into Your Power

For the past eleven years, I have been teaching Beyond Intention in various formats, leading Beyond Intention workshops all over the world, and coaching clients from all walks of life. And as you have seen, there is a genuine call for people to examine their lives so as to see how each program has a genuine cause, whether it's environmental or one in direct correlation to something that happened, so this isn't about judging you.

It's simply about highlighting one area in your life where you feel resistance. By doing the work of unpacking your resistance, you become empowered so that you are in the driver's seat—so that you are creating and directing where you want to go with your life.

One of the reasons why I believe so many people struggle to accept the idea of being in the driver's seat of their life is that *if* they're in the driver's seat of their life, then they also have to accept that they drove themselves to where they are.

So if, for instance, you hate your job or you're in an abusive relationship, you're the one who got you to it. The good news, though, is that if you drove yourself there, then you can drive yourself away. The real challenge is in stepping into your power and actually doing it. But for now, I don't want you to get too caught up in the *how* because the Beyond Intention framework is what is going to empower you to make the new choices that will effectively drive to you to your new destination.

I can tell you from my own life, that at one time or another, I created every excuse under the sun and blamed ever other person but myself for all the hard times I went through. The purposeful, abundant life I now love, and the joy and honor I feel every day in living a life of service for others only started to happen when I began accepting complete and total responsibility for my life as a whole.

By not picking and choosing the parts of the journey for which I wanted to be responsible, I could no longer pass off the blame. This forced me to accept all of it—all of the muck, the mire, the missteps, the poor choices, and so on and so on. By taking responsibility for and accepting all of my choices, I had to step into a mindset where I was the one who held power. By doing so, this enabled me to make the ongoing, deliberate choices I've made.

Regardless of third party influence, the choice is yours as to how—or even if—you choose to respond to the people or circumstances that appear in your life. That makes you not only in control of the lock/unlock button to your car, but also you have the power to kick people *out* of your car!

The moral of this story is you don't have to go through life carrying the baggage of other people, whether internally with regard to how you feel about them, or even physically, as in it's your decision as to whether or not you want them in your life or environment in any form.

Let's do another exercise.

If you feel resistance to being in the driver's seat of your life, I would like you to write down why.

Perhaps you genuinely feel as though you have someone to blame. It could also be that you don't understand the concept and it doesn't make sense to you. Or maybe you don't have any resistance and are happy to be in the driver's seat of your life, and if so, then that's great!

But if there is even the slightest bit of resistance, then go ahead and do this exercise.

For now, just jot down any resistance you feel, as well as one or two ideas why that might be so. It's not about having a correct answer, just about having ideas to work with. What we're doing is building new neural pathways—a new way of thinking that ultimately will lead to a new way of being, and that in turn will lead to new choices, which will eventually lead to your new life.

As I mentioned earlier, a microshift is a consistent series of baby steps made in the direction of a consciously chosen outcome. At a Tony Robbins event I attended five years ago, I heard him say that when a plane takes off, if it is just two degrees off its correct course, it will end up in a completely wrong place.

Don't quote me on the destinations, but if it takes off from London, and it's is supposed to be going to New York—but it's just two degrees off, it can end up in Anchorage, Alaska or Lima, Peru.

You get the point, so let's make a counterpoint and put a positive spin on this. If you make even one or two degrees of positive change in your life, you can end up in a completely new place too. This is what I want you to remember.

You may not accept everything I'm saying right now, and you may not be able to embody all of it at this moment, but that's okay. As long as you can take something from this to begin moving you in a new direction, you will start to see improvements in your life. The side effect is you will start to experience more and more joy and less and less of what you've come to know as your normal, baseline states that in some cases don't do you any good.

BEYOND INTENTION
STEP TWO: CLEAR

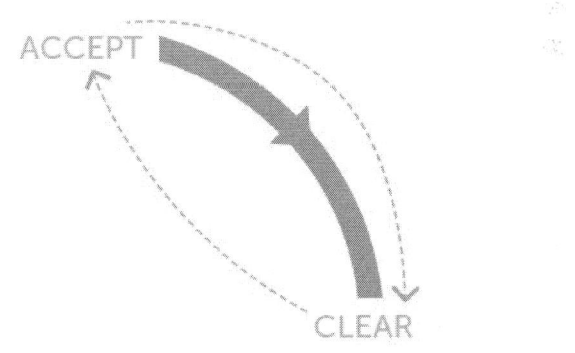

In Step One of Beyond Intention, we laid the foundation for change, and it's this:

To change your life, you need to first accept responsibility for it. Here in Step Two, you'll continue building on that foundation by taking the power you reclaimed and applying it to the only real place transformation can occur—in the now.

If you don't approach the action of clearing with total responsibility for the outcome, then you're wasting your time. I say this because I have not only seen this in my own life but in the lives of thousands of people around the globe who have been implementing Beyond Intention in their lives.

My initial recognition of the importance of clearing came as I read the words of Dr. Joe Vitale in his book, *The Key*. At that point in my life's journey, due to the work I had already been doing for many years, the methods of visualization, goal setting, and positive thinking weren't anything new to me. Yes, I regularly used these methodologies to create what externally could be deemed a successful life. But as anyone who has been following my story knows, for some reason, it stopped working.

The year was 2009, and the idea of manifesting and calling in what you desired—once an outsider's perspective—began infiltrating pop culture. Everyone was talking about feelings, the Law of Attraction, vision boards, etc. But the results were unfounded at best, not to mention not really what you'd expect from the law.

Despite proclaiming my intentions loudly, nothing was showing up—not to mention it seemed that everything in my life was falling apart. Everything was going sideways, and whenever I would try to focus my mind on something, it would actually uncreate what I was trying to create. It was crazy, and at this time I could see why so many people would say, *there's no point in trying because it will all go wrong anyway. It always does.*

Upon reading *The Secret*, I recognized the source material almost immediately. They were the exact same principles that had brought me the initial success I'd enjoyed up until that point in my life. The problem was, it wasn't working for me anymore.

Many people naturally connected to the material when they read *The Secret*.

My theory on this was proven in early 2019 when my Micro2Millions Mastermind (now just micro2millions on Beyond Intention University) first launched. The biggest leaps forward in this challenge were always gained by the people who knew the least. I believe this was because they had no preconceived notions or ideas about what 'should' be happening.

Back in 2008, however, I had no explanation as to why the same thing I had spent the preceding year doing sent my life spiraling into oblivion. Common Denominator Theory, the basis of Step One of Beyond Intention, had made its way into my life by then and so I had committed to giving life another chance. I had set aside my thoughts of suicide and even started feeling good—if not hopeful—again, yet still the results just weren't showing up.

It started that day I read Dr. Vitale's book, *The Key*. I then went on to read another book of his called *Zero Limits*, which began my journey of tying in the work of another great teacher and thought leader, Eckhart Tolle.

None of this would have meant anything, however, were it not for the owning of my personal power in Step One of Beyond Intention: Accept.

For the foundational Step Two: Clear, you may find some resistance with regard to consciously creating your new outcomes. The difference between your conscious and subconscious resistance is something we'll look at later in this book.

But for now, I want you to just stay with me as you learn the foundation, the core of which is this: you can neither create nor destroy energy; you can only change it.

Clearing is the active process of performing exercises to cut ties with the mental, emotional, and often physical baggage of the past so you can push through the places where you're stuck in your life. Said another way, it's the transmutation of energy, and you do this by transforming stuck energy into an elevated frequency/emotion—free of the baggage that holds you stagnant—as opposed to the normal practice of resistance and avoidance.

So for this exercise, what I'd like you to do is go into the feeling of resistance you examined earlier in relation to being in the driver's seat. I want you to really go into that feeling of resistance and start building a relationship with it. Then I want you to journal how that feels.

Where does resistance occur in your body? Does it have a face? Does it have a color associated? Does any imagery pop up? Often, these feelings are personified, whether by association or by assignment of blame for the existence of it as a program.

Some of my coaching clients have even told me they associate a specific taste with resistance. So any images, sensory inputs, whatever comes to you, write them in your journal. Put down this book for a moment and do the exercise now.

Seriously, do the exercise.

*   *   *

Welcome back. I wanted you to experience and become familiar with the energy and emotions of resistance because it's that resistance preventing your new life from arising. Creation only happens in the present moment, and the reason for this is that the present moment is all there really is. You cannot, after all, create from a space that doesn't exist.

According to Eckhart Tolle's work, which has now been demonstrated with peer-reviewed science all over the world, time as we have been taught it is just not real. It's an illusion held together by the false construct of numbers on our clocks and dates on our calendars.

When you have resistance, you're being pulled energetically out of the present moment into what I mentioned earlier and what we in the Beyond Intention paradigm call *energy traps*. These energy traps rob you of your power in the present moment to make conscious changes that will effect a deliberate outcome in the future. How? Because they keep you trapped *out of* the now, which is the only place in which change can be effected.

What we're going to do now is reframe the resistance that you highlighted with a new intention that you will work on as part of your homework.

Reframing and Re-educating

By the time you get through this program, you're going to have a few intentions, but while we're here together, I'd like you to stay on task and keep working and playing with your intentions in your own time. Make this a daily practice.

For now, the exercise you're going to do requires you to rewrite the intention you had in the beginning and reframe it in a positive manner. If your intention was about getting away from a particular person, place, thing, or state of being, you're not going to include them in the wording.

You're just going to talk about the positive. So it's not, *I don't want stress in my life.* Think about the opposite of stress and write an intention around the opposite state. That would be, *My life is peaceful and at ease.*

So what is the state of being that you'd like to be in? Instead of saying, *I don't want to be broke anymore,* reframe that statement with abundance. If you want wealth, give it some clarity. What does your ideal life look like with all that wealth? How much money do you need to live in that life? If there's a sickness you want to get through, then don't talk about the sickness. Talk about health. One I often use is: *I'm in perfect health. All is well with my mind, body, and soul.*

So go ahead, take another break, and use as much time as you need. Have another crack at rewriting your intention in a positive framework. Close your eyes, run a mental picture of how your life would be if your intention came to fruition, and write down how it feels and the associated emotions.

Yes, now!

Energy is such a funny phrase. When I first started hearing about all of this energy malarkey, it made me think of energy companies—you know, the people that sell electricity, gas, solar, and so on. That's when I started to do more research, which slowly gave me a deeper understanding of the nature of reality, especially as to how the universe really works. While I understood the ideas behind creating from thought, I hadn't really dug into the science behind it.

Growing up in school, we were always taught that the reality we experienced was made up of matter, and of how matter was made up of atoms. The atom was supposed to be the smallest piece of matter that existed. And then physicists found subatomic particles. What scientists are now saying is that when they opened up these atoms and subatomic particles, they found out that 99.9999999% of it was actually energy.

So the atom wasn't anything physical. Rather, what appeared to be empty space was actually energy. So, if 99.9999999% of the building blocks of what we understand to be physical matter is empty space, that means 99.9999999% of what we call reality is actually energy.

This completely blew my mind, especially when I started learning about how the quantum model also reveals that this energy not only displays an intelligence, but also responds entirely to how it is observed.

That energy, when observed, actually collapses into physical matter. So if you really drill down to the energy forming these atoms, it's actually in flux. It's doesn't form into anything physical until an observation collapses it into a particular pattern, but we're going to talk more about that later in the book.

Quite early in my teaching career, on my first speaking and teaching tour, I was getting ready to do an early Beyond Intention workshop in Los Angeles. With a free day before teaching, I decided to fly from L.A. to San Jose with the plan of connecting to the energy of nature. I wanted to see the great Redwoods of Northern California.

Because they are so old, I was told they possessed an energetic knowing that could viscerally be felt, and that as you walked amongst them, if you took a moment to go inward, you could really connect with the spirit of the earth. When I arrived, surrounded by trees more than one thousand years old, I found the perfect site to ground myself and settle in for the night in preparation to teach the following day.

The first thing I noticed was that the energy around these old trees was very different. I decided to do a walking meditation, and as I did, I visualized myself connecting with the history of the Earth. It was magic... until thoughts of my current relationship challenges interrupted the silence.

Aware of my thoughts, I immediately caught the attempted interruption of the noisy chatter of my mind—and smiled. It was at this moment, however, that the gremlins of the mind attempted to secure foothold. As they did, my mind went back to my previous girlfriend and laid out the case that my ex-girlfriend never created the drama and upset that my current girlfriend was creating.

For about thirty seconds, I lost control of the wheel and slipped back in time to my former relationship that never had the particular challenges of my current one. Musing on how peaceful and free this former relationship had been, I bathed in the happy memories, the laughter, etc., only to catch myself as the vision became stronger.

Consciousness cannot be in two places at the same time, so in this instance, my connection to nature, as well as my capacity to send loving energy to my girlfriend was blocked by my consciousness residing in time past. For a short time, I was happily held captive by a past reflection that was not even as rosy as I had painted it.

Earlier, when playing with the choice machine, we came to the logical conclusion that outcomes were changed by new choices. But when we are stuck in the same thought loops making all the same unconscious choices, all we do is perpetuate the same outcomes.

Sometimes, the anchor of those thought loops is so tied to memories of the past that we are blinded to the possibilities available to us in the present. And sometimes, we are so stuck in the fear or excitement of a possible future that we are no longer present in the moment—which is where we make new choices to create new outcomes.

One aspect of the energy trap that's sometimes lost on my clients or students is the notion that what traps them must be something negative.

In this case, it was actually happy memories that had trapped me. Exaggeratedly so, but still—traps are traps. Anything that pulls your consciousness away from the now is a trap disempowering you from effecting change in the only place that is real, the now.

To be in heart, coherence is one of the most natural states of presence, and when you're in the present moment, there are no stories, narratives, or belief systems at play. Just the now, and in that space, you can create anything you want, but you don't necessarily have to use Heart Coherence to get into that state of creation.

As you start to take stock of those times in your life when you have actually been in heart coherence, or even close to it, even if it's just for a moment, this is actually a guidepost to what will serve you most as your clearing toolkit, which as you know is what we are developing in this book. For me, meditation is the most prevalent daily activity I perform to get coherent and present to the here and now, which is exactly why I start every day with it.

I also have times in the day where I check in so as to keep myself in balance. This serves to check in with my state of being and to check where my mind is. I do this by setting alarms throughout the day. I set alarms for 9 a.m., 11a.m., 2 p.m., and 5 p.m., and when they go off, I take a moment to move into heart coherence. Sometimes, I do breathwork from my yoga practice. If I have more time, I may also do a short meditation. It's all about anchoring in and making your default setting more and more aligned with being present.

Meditation and yoga are very important daily practices for me to get present and heart coherent. I also find I am very present when playing the piano. For some people, it's going for a run. For others, it's cleaning. Another friend gets really present mowing the lawn and doing yard work. That's his meditation. There are so many everyday tasks that can get you into a state of presence, so let's do an exercise to do just that.

For this exercise, I want you to go all in. To begin, I'd like you to journal about when you feel most disengaged from the present.

Is there an exercise, action, or activity that you do? Or do certain people pull you out of the present moment? Is there a physical space or environment that does this? Is there a particular thought that comes into your being that does this? Take 24 hours to log all of this in your journal—your relationship with the present moment, when you're out of sync, and when you are present in it. This will support you in creating a model, showing you how you are able to deliberately return to the present moment as a conscious choice. Even if it's just for a short while.

Your Personal Clearing Toolkit

At this point, we're going to take getting present one step further by building your personal clearing toolkit. This is a big and important step in work, so again I'm going to need you to commit to really honoring yourself and standing in your integrity by following through with these exercises. It is only by doing the work that you'll get the results.

So let's bring up two things that we've played with so far. First, I want you to bring up your original intention. Second, bring up the list of blocks that you previously identified. It is important to identify and have these blocks and points of resistance written down. You will win the battle against your demons not so much in the fight, but in treating them as the vampires that they are—by shining the light of awareness on them.

As you also go deeper into Beyond Intention, I want to point out that although Step One of the paradigm is mostly autonomous, this doesn't mean you shouldn't find support as you grow and do the work. From time to time, I have mistakenly been seen as advocating going it alone and not taking help, including more traditional modalities such as therapy. This, however, is not at all what I teach or even practice.

My life, quite literally, was saved by therapy.

Were it not for the amazing Dr. Helen McKewen, the person who properly diagnosed my Asperger's, to this day I may still have been pinned under the weight of the crippling anxiety that held me captive. And to this very day, I am still actively supported by a powerful team of coaches, teachers, and lightworkers. It is these angels who empower me to show up the way I do for you all every day.

The important thing is that you recognize support is a joint effort and collaboration, but recognize that the collaboration still has you in the driver's seat. This means the results or outcomes of this joint effort still hold you solely responsible for your life.

It's time to apply all that you've learned so far so you can build your own personal clearing toolkit—a toolkit that works for you, your own unique experiences, personality, and the type of energy traps and baseline states that you want to work through.

Clearing may involve some deep diving into yourself. With a few of my coaching clients, I've seen some really deep energy traps that sometimes have been decades in the making. These instances may be better supported by something more disruptive—for example, by changing your physiology through dance.

Some instances of thought loops and horrific traumas individuals have seen have been embedded from a really young age. I want to stress once more that having the right support when moving through some of these energy traps can be very beneficial. But keep playing with the tools in this book, keep finding your edges, and use your journal practice to record your growth.

In our coaching practice and retreats, we have the time and space to really hold a client's hand through this process. In the Clearing Encyclopedia section featured in the appendices is an array of tools you can draw upon to feel more supported in their transformation.

We also have relationships with many of the global thought leaders whose tools are featured in the encyclopedia, and you will find interviews with some on the Do it with Dan Podcast.

None of the support we offer, though, means anything unless you do the work and recognize these traps for what they truly are—an ephemeral blip in infinity in which the potential exists for it to be transcended.

At this time in the process and before you move on, I'd like to remind you again to be gentle with yourself. You have spent an entire lifetime building the state of being that comprises who you are today. It could be that your attention is being blocked by one of the deep energy traps I mentioned earlier. In that case, it would have been formed a very, very long time ago and may require time to unfold.

If that's your belief system, the work is required every day, and you must remain all in, keeping track of your progress so that you can celebrate it, all the while inviting more of that same positive transformational energy into your life.

"If you're doing everything right, then nothing is going wrong."

The idea that when you're doing everything right, nothing should be going wrong—and that everything should be manifesting just the way you asked for it—can be a little confusing. Many times in life, when you do the work, the results do not show up immediately.

This does not mean you should despair. Sometimes, it only means that you need to change your mindset because a microshift in thinking can be that powerful. Once you think about it, you create it. The trick is that in the space between thinking and being is where the creation occurs. For clarity, refer to the flow funnel earlier in the book.

When you believe that something is going to happen, it happens. Whatever you decide to create consciously or subconsciously, it is mandatory that you believe in it first. The reason why sometimes our creations don't happen is that our belief systems have created a single road upon which it must happen.

The illusion of linear time sometimes causes people to believe there must be a certain amount of time that needs to occur between when they set our intentions and the intention showing up. Some people have a fantasy that they must work in a certain way to get what they want, but first, they must align their belief system with their thoughts. For instance, when one believes that they are going to make a big sum of money, their thoughts must be in alignment with the way they need to work for it.

It is essential to shift your belief system definitively to reflect what you want, as well as how you want things to show up for you. Suppose you believe that in relationships it is hard to cope, or you can't find the right partner. If this is the belief, then this is what will happen because you perceive the relationship through this lens; thus, this is exactly what will be reflected back to you.

So the key is to not live as if something is *going* to happen, but instead, live as though what you want has *already* happened.

This process consistently imprints a new way of being upon you until the time comes when you actually *become* what you desire. Thus, the key is that if you want something, there has to be an alignment to your belief system.

The other side of this coin is that if you know that working is your belief, then hold the frequency, and work till you get it. If time is a big hurdle for you, introduce practices in patience while the inevitable comes to you along the river of time.

You will, if these or any other beliefs are yours, be better served by working with them, even if you are at the same time working on expanding beyond their limitations.

Recap: Tying It All Together So You Can Move into Your Future

Now I want you to take a moment to recap where you are with your intention, to show you how this all ties together.

In Step One, I outlined that you are the creator of everything showing up in your life right now, and that it's only through changing your choices about your state of being that you can allow for change. This puts the responsibility on you to enact those changes, thus creating the new life you truly want for yourself.

I also outlined the way that change comes through new choices, leading to new outcomes.

Finally, I detailed how those choices can only effectively be made in the present moment, and that to get back to that moment, you will need to do the work of clearing the energy traps that keep you captive either in the past or in an imagined, anxiety-inducing future.

Our personal clearing toolkit allows you to come back to the present moment, the only place in which you can create change. It's important to be gentle with yourself throughout this process and to stick to your commitment to live life on your terms—a life with more joy, not one tied to the disempowering belief systems that brought you to where you currently are along your life's journey.

With this in mind and returning to your original intention, I invite you to play with the idea of being responsible for your *new* outcomes. Play with the beauty of the reality in which only you allow other people to dictate, influence, or impede your outcome *because you allowed them to do it.* Thus you can also allow them *not* to do it. Play with the power that this gives you to create the life you want.

Play with the clearing tools that you now have in your possession. Play with the exercises you've done so far that identify which tools actually get you into the present moment. Step back to the present moment simply because you've chosen to enjoy the feeling of being present—since the present is a place where there are no stories, no narratives, and no energy traps.

The purpose of Beyond Intention is to achieve self-mastery over your state of being, and with that power, create what your heart desires. From this space, you can deliberately delve beyond the limitations of our past programs. You can create joy, and you can enjoy the beauty of a fully embodied 3D experience—no matter what your beliefs are about what happens next.

In our *Create Your Ideal Life* and *Ideal Life Blueprint* online programs, we specifically work on outlining and creating a roadmap to a specific vision for your life, while in *Beyond Success* we take this approach into the corporate world and the world of entrepreneurship.

At this moment in your journey, there exists the opportunity for you to experience wholeness, joy, happiness, and love. And with that in mind, I'd like you to get ready for Step Three.

Here, you will begin to connect to the specific outcome as a physical experience in the here and now, drawing on that energy to become a magnet for what you intend to create.

BEYOND INTENTION
STEP THREE: GRATITUDE

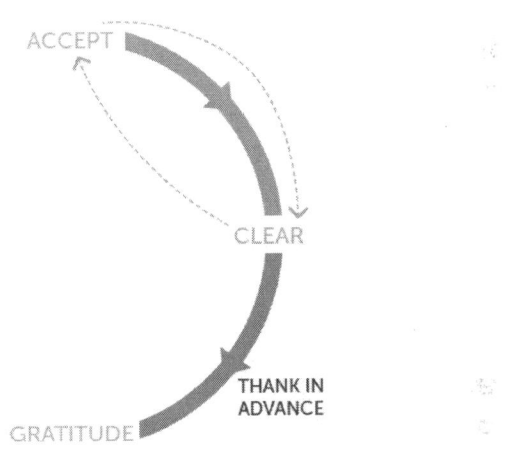

Before you begin this chapter, take a moment to celebrate making it this far. By now, you should have a growing list of intentions. As you probably discovered, when you set your initial intention, you began to identify some of the traps and baseline states of being surrounding it.

But don't let that get you flustered. Stay on course with your primary intention. When the frustrations and fears build up, get clear on what you're trying to create and pull yourself back to the present. All of these reactions are just the autopilot deep within assuming control of the wheel, calling for you to come back to what it understands, knows, and is familiar with. It's just doing its job, so know there is no enemy inside your mind. All it's doing is regurgitating what was programmed, simply following the orders it's been given.

There is no problem here and all you need to do is start programming your mind another way.

The Beyond Intention paradigm empowers you to decide what instructions you give that system, and to change them. Done properly, this internal guidance system starts producing the outcomes and results that you deliberately and consciously chose, as opposed to just following an automatic program that, in most cases, was set, created, and programmed completely outside of your awareness.

As you move into the power of gratitude, Step Three of the Beyond Intention paradigm, please just stay with your initial intention.

You see, I really want you to remain focused in terms of energy and intention, giving you a rhythm of success to implement in other life areas, creating new outcomes in the days, weeks, months, and years ahead.

The Intersection of Gratitude and Quantum Physics

Given how things work in the world, you might think gratitude is where you give thanks for your intention successfully coming to fruition, but that's not actually how it works in this instance. Gratitude is the place in which the intention is born.

Perhaps by this point in the process of applying Beyond Intention in your life, you are thinking, *okay, there's a missing link here. I've done the clearing, done what I'm supposed to do, and yet my intention still hasn't shown up.*

Does that sound like you? Have you been telling yourself you're struggling with the exercises?

Some of you may have even found this as an opportunity to start beating yourself up, telling yourself that you've failed or that you didn't perform the process correctly. Well, hold your horses. We're actually still in the process of creating the outcome, and gratitude is where it's really born.

It dawned on me once that there is quite a fine line between faith and fear. The more I thought about it, the more I realized that the lines came down to perception.

The fear you have—that something you don't want to happen will occur—can be so strong that simply imagining that future can have significant negative effects in the present—especially on your stress levels. When it comes to your fear of this future event, the emotion attached to it leads to anxiety, which means living in an imaginary future you don't want. This brings you to live in that unwanted state of anxiety—and yet the thing you dread has not even come to pass!

With faith, however, that future event is actually *something you want.*

So you see, both sides of this coin involve future events affecting your present state, and both are based on a perception about an imaginary future.

Now let's take gratitude as one of the foundations of the Beyond Intention paradigm. Gratitude is the most powerful tool for creating a positive outcome in your life because as a state of being, it's a reflection of the fact that what you have spent your energy creating will come to fruition.

In this respect, faith is a natural feeling of expectancy.

As I stated earlier, it's important to understand the connection between observation and reality. While I'm no quantum physicist, nor is Scott Sunderland, author of *Finding Ugly*, there's something about the description he shares that makes understanding quantum physics a lot easier to grasp.

'In 2002, a group of researchers set up the experiment again with a better understanding of quantum physics to try and get a grasp of what quantum physics really is. Very simply put, the experiment showed the reaction of what happens when little particles of matter were shot at a board with two slits in it. Imagine a sheet of plywood with 2 vertical slits, both maybe 6" wide by 36" long, cut a few feet apart from each other, in the center of the plywood. Now imagine hitting tennis balls at the plywood. If the balls hit the plywood and not the slits or the openings, they would just bounce back, right? The balls will only go past the plywood if they get hit through the slits. Now let's say there was a screen behind the plywood. The screen would get marked by a tennis ball every time one made it through either slit. You would most likely conclude that the shapes that were created on the screen, after all the balls went through, would be in the same shapes as the slits on the plywood, right? That there would be 2 slits on the screen that mirrored the slits on the plywood. Are you following this so far? But instead of shooting tennis balls through plywood, they shot subatomic particles, or electrons, at a sort of board with much smaller slits in it. Each time an electron made it through one of the slits, it made a mark on the screen behind it and created the same double slit shapes, as they expected it to.

Now, this is where it got really funky. They recorded the electrons as they were shot at the board. As you would expect, after a period of time, the screen was all marked up in the shape of the two slits from the board in front where some of the electrons made it through when recording the experiment. But the funky part? The researchers then decided to let the machine run without recording it or watching it. When they came back at the conclusion of the experiment, what do you think showed up on the screen? You would think that the screen would be marked in the shape of the two slits as it was before, right? After all, the only difference was the recording. But nope, that's not at all what happened. The screen was covered with marks, and not just where the slits were, but everywhere. What was the difference? Everything remained the same except there was no one and nothing watching the electrons. No observer. The scientists concluded that it was the observer that made the difference. That when no one was watching, the electrons turned into possibility. So, in other words, with no one watching the electrons, they created random patterns that were not what you would expect, the observer you. You would expect the pattern to be in the shape of the slits, but when you weren't there to put that intention, or thought, on the electrons, they all turned into possibility.

What does all this mean? By the observer, or you, watching the electrons, it affected how they acted. The observers' thought, or intention, of how the electron would behave and land on the screen, made the electron land in the shape of the slit. It was actually thought, by the observer, that created the pattern. The thought or intentions of the researchers that were conducting the experiment. Take them out of the equation, and the electron became anything, anywhere, or everything, everywhere. It became all possible. And that's exactly why there was no pattern of the slits. There was no thought or intention placed on them to make that pattern. Get it? Quantum Physics at its basics."

Scott's really smart and has the biggest heart. I love him to bits, and I'm so grateful for his explanation of the experiment. It allows those of us not so scientifically oriented to start building a model of understanding that will support what we are exploring in this book.

Don't get me wrong, I am well aware of the simplification of this explanation and have gone to great lengths to get a deeper understanding of it myself. I have also sat with physicists to try to gain a better understanding of it all, but for the purpose of this book and keeping it light and accessible, let's stick with this explanation.

I want to thank Scott for giving me the opportunity to share this excerpt from his book. I encourage you to grab a copy of *Finding Ugly* on Amazon. Scott is also the founder of the Freedom Project, which you can find online.

With that said, let's start connecting the dots between Scott's explanation of how electrons work and what I previously said about fear, faith, and the foundation of gratitude in Beyond Intention.

Gratitude as a Way of Life

I'd like you to think back to our earlier discussion about atoms being 99.9999% energy.

I'm going to give you a second to let that penny drop.

Has the coin hit the floor yet?

I really want you to connect to the magic of this idea; what you observe is dictated by your attention, or more to the point, by your thoughts.

Your thoughts are the observations of the mind—intentions you set consciously or unconsciously—and it is these thoughts that set the wheels of creation in motion. Ultimately, your external experience is dictated by the alignment (or lack thereof) to that observation with your feelings, beliefs, and actions. Another way of saying this is you instruct those electrons as to how to show up in your life!

In this step of Beyond Intention, you are therefore going to reset your expectations. You're going to hack the system so that the expectation around your intention becomes a positive manifestation of the outcome that you're seeking to manifest. Said more simply—in this step of Beyond Intention, you're going to hack the system so that your intention is not guided by the slits of your existing program.

You're going to guide the intention to the backdrop in the pattern that you want, irrespective of the slits in the board, and you're going to do that by experiencing gratitude for its fruition in advance of it happening.

Before we move on, I'd like you to quickly do another exercise. I'd like you to go ahead and say two words out loud right now: "Thank you."

Now I'd like you to close your eyes and bring up a memory of a time when you were really grateful for something or someone in your life. Go ahead and really dive deep into the memory.

Notice how you feel right now as you experience that memory. A big part of our work is that 'gratitude' is more than a word. It's a feeling. Gratitude is an energetic signature, which, when tapped into, is the ultimate power source for the creation of what you imagine.

How does gratitude do this?

Well, when you have sufficient faith in the possibility of something being the likely outcome, the probability of the outcome you observe into existence goes through the roof. It does so by literally making you a magnet to those experiences that you desired and observed into your life. Your expectation guides the thought, which calls those electrons onto the backboard in the pattern that you have consciously and deliberately chosen.

In terms of the Beyond Intention paradigm, gratitude is a way of life. When you build an attitude of gratitude that consistently expects the best, you reduce the resistance from your subconscious belief systems by programming it with real-world experiences. This is how you create a positive loop of expecting the best, and when you do that, the best shows up for you, one success at a time. As you transform your subconscious mind into new positive thought patterns, one of the success measures is knowing that what you're creating is going to show up.

Now return to your intention and let's go through the steps once again. You have accepted that the manifestation of this intention is your sole responsibility and you've cleared the energy around your past. This is going to allow you to tap into the power of the present moment so you can make new choices not governed by your subconscious programs.

Following Step Two of Beyond Intention, you should be in the present moment, clear of the stories, clear of the belief systems, and clear of all the narratives which impede this intention from coming into being. This doesn't mean stories won't still resurface. It means by hacking the system and stepping into the present moment, you create the space for this intention to show up.

By now you should have taken some time to play with the clearing tools, so I would like you to select one. As an example, I would suggest checking out heart coherence on the free resources page of www.dreamwithdan.com.

If you chose heart coherence, stay in this feeling for a moment. In the beauty of this infinite Now, I'd like you to really imagine just what it will feel like for your intention to be a part of your life when it shows up for you.

How will you feel? What were your experiences in life? Deeply and meaningfully connect with the feelings and emotions as this is what successfully creates the outcome.

Once your creation comes to fruition, picture the celebration. Run the mental images of who you will tell and how. Close your eyes, really feel into it, and hold that feeling. When you have it locked down, when you have really brought all of your senses into a connection with every energetic inch of that metaphysical experience, gently open your eyes and jot down the top four or five emotions that you felt in association with the success.

You just experienced the magic of being grateful in advance of the outcome. What I'd like you to do now is whenever you think about your intention, go back to that feeling—that feeling you just experienced in heart coherence with your eyes closed. Use this shortlist of the top four or five emotions and feelings that you associate with the intention. Think of it almost like an emotional script you need to follow and run through in order to really connect with your vision.

When you connect with the vision of something ahead of time, you've created it with your being. There is some sexy science around this, but in short, you are tapping into what some scientists refer to as a 'Quantum Potential.'

Because you've had the thought, it's become a part of you by imprinting in your emotional body.

You see, the mind does not know the difference between the physical experience of the outcome showing up and the emotional experience that you have by imagining it.

For the purpose of this exercise and bringing this power into your life, I beg you for the sake of your own greater good to give this a try. As you do, write down any resistance, then create an intention around that resistance being shifted when it arises.

If you're doing things the same way you've always done them, you're going to keep getting the same results, so you might as well try something different. Otherwise, nothing is going to change, is it?

Doing things the way you've done them so far hasn't been working out too well for you, so it's time to give Quantum Potential a shot!

The Reticular Activating System

According to the textbook of clinical neurology, 2007 edition, the reticular activating system (R.A.S.) is:

> 'A network of neurons located in the brain stem that project anteriorly to the hypothalamus to mediate behavior, as well as both posteriorly to the Thalamus and directly to the cortex for activation of awake desynchronized cortical EEG patterns.'

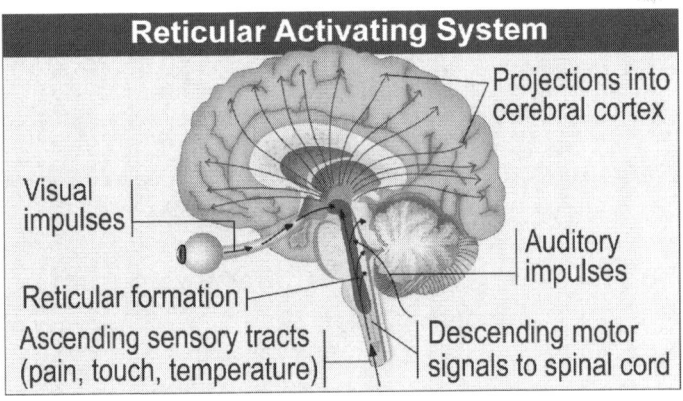

Well, that sounds like a whole bunch of nothing to the layman. Instead, I like an excerpt I found on study. com, which translates that idea into non-scientific English:

> 'While it may be a fairly small part of your brain, the RAS has a very important role: it's the gatekeeper of information that is let into the conscious mind. This little bit of brain matter is responsible for filtering the massive amounts of information your sensory organs are constantly throwing at it and selecting the ones that are most important for your conscious mind to pay attention to.'

By now, I hope you see how this part of the brain might be pretty useful in creating

an environment for the realization of your intentions; it acts as a filter, and most importantly, it is a filter that *you can program intentionally.*

As I mentioned earlier, gratitude is a way of life. I've already given you some hacks to keep the clearing momentum going, which should facilitate you to create new outcomes in your physical reality.

The goal, however, is for this become your norm, and to make gratitude your subconscious program, your default mode of creation.

For our coaching clients, especially those in our mastermind programs, the aim is to truly get beyond the setting of intentions. By getting present to your intention, you *become* it, training your conscious program to be one of acceptance.

Now you can become present at will, and in turn, create the tendency to gravitate toward expecting positive outcomes—the outcomes you've chosen to manifest because that's just what you do now.

Changing Your Programs for the Long Term

Science reveals that there are three principal avenues for effectively changing our programs for the long term.

Number one is accessing theta brainwave patterns. We do this in Beyond Intention through tools such as hypnosis, Neurolinguistic Programming, and other such techniques. I also have a number of guided visualization audios available online, including free material in the free resources section of www.dreamwithdan.com. These audio files are designed to affect several levels of the mind when choosing new states of being.

The second practice for creating long-term change is practice and repetition, which is especially effective when accessing alpha brainwaves, correlating to being in a state of relaxed awareness, another level of the mind served by the guided visualizations. A great program I'd like to recommend to you is the Silva Method, by Jose Silva who does some great work with alpha brainwaves.

A company whose products has been instrumental in supporting my journey for more than twenty years is Learning Strategies Corporation. I highly recommend their products, and on my website, you will find some of my suggested tools on offer from Learning Strategies Corporation. Having personally completed a lot of their programs in terms of using alpha brainwaves to create new patterns of behavior, Learning Strategies Corporation is a company I trust.

Perhaps the most effective tool I have found in terms of creating change, I will share with you right now. This may also prove to be one of the most effective in helping you build your new mindset. Are you ready?

Quit complaining.

Seriously. Quit complaining.

That's it!

In case you hadn't realized it, complaining is the complete antithesis to gratitude, and by allowing complaining to be a part of your life, you allow your reticular activating system to see more things to complain about. But if you instead look for things to be grateful for—*and* rest your attention on them—you make yourself a magnet for more positive experiences.

Why? Because if that's what you are observing more of in your life, that's what will show up for you. With that being said, you're going to institute a new regime into your life, and that is to start keeping a gratitude journal.

Over the course of the day, I want you to look for just three things to be grateful for. That's not too hard, right? If you have more, that's fine, but before going to bed, you need to write down at least three things you are grateful for.

When you're done, look at your list, then close your eyes and take a moment or two to connect with the feeling of gratitude for what you just wrote in your journal. In the morning when you wake up, review what you wrote, close your eyes, and connect with those feelings again.

The most important part of this exercise is that whatever you put on your list, it should generate a feeling of gratitude. This is the difference between just saying thank you habitually and *feeling* thankful. So really connect with that genuine feeling of gratitude for this experience.

There's a second part of this exercise, however. The first is taking just one day—just 24 hours—to refrain from complaining. This includes complaints about yourself, and backdoor complaints about people. If you slip up, don't fret or beat yourself up. Just journal what you complained about. Make the conscious decision to be more aware next time, and keep going until you get there.

BEYOND INTENTION
STEP FOUR: LISTEN

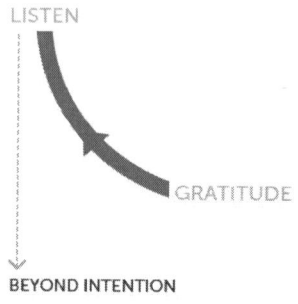

My girlfriend had grown increasingly and understandably concerned with my running off to the States. Every month or two, I would head off to another meditation retreat, each time coming back with a bigger tribe of new people to whom I was connected and with whom I was in divine love.

Admittedly, if the roles were reversed, and I had seen her go from just a half dozen close friends all of her life to dozens of new people—many of them men with whom she constantly shared time and energy, and in which she messaged them about how much she loved them—I too would have had some concerns.

Thankfully, however, she eventually traveled to one of these community events with me and met many of the people I'd come to love. Over time, she finally began understanding what this newfound sense of love and connection was and that I was not having inappropriate connections with these people. I had also not been sucked into a cult!

Due to challenges of varying degrees, including some with regard to she and I coming from different cultures and hers not accepting outsiders, our relationship ended. The relationship for which I had given up my dream life was doomed, in part because of the color of my skin.

In truth, there had been a disconnect from the beginning, one that didn't make sense until we had the honest conversations that led to our ending. As words were said that could not be taken back, and truths made known that she rightly guessed I might struggle to get past, we went our separate ways.

What was crazy about the whole situation was that my relationship pattern would have continued to prevent me from enjoying the true depths of a loving connection. I would have stayed in the relationship, telling myself that there was work I needed to do on myself, robbing me of my truth and keeping me playing small and unfulfilled in this area of my life.

The day that this unconscious program came to the surface was a good day. I was in Florida to share my work and staying with a friend from the community. I had left Mexico, where I was living at the time, on good terms (or so I thought) with a deeply honest conversation that I hoped would give way to healing.

It was my suggestion we end, given the truth that had come to light, another in a year-long series of attempts to end on good terms. I had repeatedly sought counsel and coaching with regard to this relationship, although I would later learn the counseling was mostly about me receiving accolades for what I "had to put up with" in the relationship.

Since leaving the UK to follow my path, we had for months been housesitting, airbnbing, and living in hotels. On this particular trip, I then went to work with the intention of, at last, surprising her with a home to call our own. She had put up with a lot of moving around, and I knew that she was not really suited for the hobo lifestyle that we were living at the time.

My friend Julissa will always have a special place in my heart for many reasons, but alerting me to this one slip of unconscious thought brought new light to me in a big way. One glass of wine and one single sentence spoke it all: "You can't have everything in a relationship," I said.

"What did you say?" she replied speedily.

I played the sentence back in my mind, and all at once, the light of truth shone on a world of bullshit in which I had been hiding. I had been harming myself through my relationship, unaware that I believed love was a lie and that nobody was ever really happy outside of the Hollywood screens. I checked my Macro Intention pillars—a tool that we teach in our *Ideal Life Blueprint* online program—and my mind movie which is a type of moving vision board, and realized there was only one measly reference to my relationship...and it was pathetic at best.

I had done zero work toward calling in a healthy, nourishing relationship, and that was reflected back to me in a life of failed relationships. All my romantic relationships had been more or less doomed for one reason or another, sometimes being made known later rather than sooner. When I realized this, with regard to my understanding of romantic relationships at that point in my life, I could not help but feel gratitude for not having brought a child into the madness I had created.

Within a week of the last conversation my ex and I had, I received the strangest text from my mother telling me that my ex had come to collect her things, which meant she had left Mexico without telling me she was returning to the UK.

I tried to call and ask her why she hadn't let me know about the trip, but my call went unanswered. When I attempted to reach out to her on my WhatsApp phone app, I also realized she'd blocked me. When I checked our social media connections, I had been blocked there too, and unfollowed by her and her friends—and a few of *mine* as well.

Over the years we'd been together, for one reason or another, I had never left the relationship. But it was the internal work I had done that week—toward aligning myself to the new frequency of love being real, and of deserving to be happy and feel expanded and nourished in a relationship—that finally shook my life free of the people, places, and things no longer aligning with this new frequency.

Patience, Shifts, and Outcomes

By now, you may already be seeing shifts in line with the new responsibility you're taking toward the creation of new outcomes and experiences in your life. You now have the tools to get present and to undo the stuck and stagnant energetic states in your life.

Your intention may not have shown up yet, and that's absolutely fine, but you *will* start seeing changes. Why?

Because you have made a commitment to begin doing things differently and making new choices. You are changing your internal states, and that will be reflected in your external life.

If you're on the path of deeper clearing work, you will start seeing shifts in how your clearings are taking hold, and these effects should be supercharged. Why? Because you are starting to realize that it's you making the changes. You're not expecting a miracle from anything outside of yourself. You are remembering that you actually *are* the miracle.

Through new feelings, new beliefs, and actions, as you keep digging deeper and connecting from intention more deliberately and consistently to your new out-come, things will begin to shift. We experience only that to which we are a vibrational match, and when you do this work, the old matches fall away as your vibration changes.

You're going to be more effective because every time you step into the space to do the work on your personal growth, you step into a more empowered way of being. You're becoming the author and creator of your life. You may have already started to see your intentions being made manifest, or maybe you haven't.

Either way, whether your creation is here and now or just around the corner, as long as you continue to do the work of allowing it to be yours, it will be yours. Part of that work is being aware of when you veer off course. You'll gain this awareness through listening.

We're now going to practice stepping into the awareness of listening, followed up by celebrating when your intention is born.

In the last chapter, you looked at the nature of reality, as well as how you imprint through observation your picture of life on reality.

For foundational point 'Step Four: Listen', no matter what you read, watch, or listen to, unless you learn to listen to yourself, you will not be able to identify where the winds of change are blowing in your life.

Very rarely does change hold unless it's acknowledged and celebrated, and progress can be celebrated and acknowledged only when you take the time out to witness it.

In this Listening step, you are going to observe, allow, and celebrate your intention as it births its way into your life. Much like my experience of love and relationship opened me up to shift my frequency to create new experiences, *listening* enables you to create a space to clear out the last of your resistance so you can move forward effortlessly toward your intended outcome.

The Receiving Mode: Holding the Frequency with Beyond Intention

I will now take you through how the Beyond Intention paradigm can help you get into what people like Abraham Hicks and others call the *receiving mode*—the optimal state of moving from intention, to creation, to manifest.

This exercise will shine some light on *how* this step of Beyond Intention creates a connection to your intention.

As I said earlier, I designed this paradigm to break through stagnant and stuck states, so you can make shifts that will take you from where you are to where you'd like to go.

As you will have seen over and over again on this journey, as soon as you have a thought in your mind, that very second it becomes a "real" thing, albeit not yet physically made manifest. As long as you don't get in the way of that though, it will be made physically manifest and show up in your life, just like every single thing in your life right now.

Note that in our time spent looking at the Beyond Intention Flow Funnel, we saw that on the journey from thought to a level of density that we can experience with our senses, resistance can and often does pop up along the way. Our beliefs are key here, and so unless you genuinely hold the belief that your new car will "poof" out of nowhere, then it won't. Period.

So far in this book, you have explored how to create internal alignment with your intention. Much of our work with Beyond Intention is about translating that internal alignment into our external experience, and we do this by holding the frequency of change as a deliberate choice. In preparation for moving forward, let's do a quick recap of what we've learned up to this point.

In 'Step One: Accept', you deliberately and consciously accept that you and you alone—through the power of the choice machine—decide what does and does not show up in your life. This may be a conscious or unconscious choice, but it does not negate you being solely responsible. This step is all about getting into the mindset of accepting that the thing you've decided you're going to create is going to show up in your life. Therefore, it's your responsibility to bring it into existence.

'Step Two: Clearing', is about getting present—coming back to the now—because it's only from the now that you have the power to create anything to show up in your life. Whenever you step out of the present moment, you give away your power in relation to the creation. Why? Because without your input, the control of the choice machine reverts back to unconscious patterns.

'Step Three: Gratitude', is about an attitude of gratitude. Said another way, it's about internally experiencing and feeling gratitude for the fruition of your intention before it shows up in your life. The idea is that there exists a reality where what you want already exists, so you just have to connect with its frequency to bring it into being.

'Step Four: Listen', addresses what you can do in the time between your creation and manifestation. That lag time may exist because you need to shed stories or illusions; these may represent resistance to experiencing your intention in your reality *now*. Mark my words, after more than a decade of using and teaching this tool, if your creation does not show up immediately, then there is most certainly something to listen to!

In short, what you are invited to witness is that all things that can happen, have happened, or will happen are all just potential outcomes waiting for you to direct energy in the name of something called 'collapsing the waveform.'

Everything is energy, measurably so, and just waiting for your instruction as to what physical form it will take. This embodiment of form happens when you "observe" it, and through that observation, you give it a blueprint for the energy to follow. In Beyond Intention, we link this to the expectation of what *will* show up in life.

So you can be grateful for your intended outcome in advance, because technically speaking, nothing is *in advance*—it's already here, waiting for you to create it by expecting it to show up. Making a choice to do so means letting go of the stories that tell you that you cannot expect it, or you're not powerful enough to create it.

By stepping into a deep and profound sense of gratitude for your creation *as if it were already physically here* is the ultimate energetic space to create an outcome.

So long as you are subject to the illusion of time, it will continue to take time to build the attitude of gratitude, but once you hold the vibration of gratitude ahead of the event, you create a funnel from the outcome directly to you.

This led us to two questions:

1. If you are connecting to the outcome now, then why do you need another step?
2. Why, when you have been doing the work, is your outcome not here?

When I have spoken so confidently about this being a law based in science, these are valid questions. The answer was given to you as we discussed the flow funnel earlier, for it is the mental environment and the belief system that form the gateway to experience.

One of the strongest collective agreements we hold as the human race is the illusion of time, and most of the delay in creation I have witnessed over the last nearly twenty years has been tied to this in some way. Because of this, a big reason why people might not see the instant manifestation of their intentions is that they just do not believe it is possible for it to show up here and now.

For this and many of the other reasons, resistance to intention makes its way through the flow funnel. This is why Step Three is so important, and why Step Three is really where the magic happens.

Again, it could be said that people don't actually 'create' anything, and they just connect to what already awaits them.

If the Quantum Model holds true, however, then we are constantly collapsing energy around us. This is the reality we see every day. It just so happens that we have a blueprint that the mind is using to inform energy at an unconscious level, and belief systems in that same unconscious part of the human mind dictate what will make its way into a person's physical world.

What you are doing via Beyond Intention is informing your consciousness to have a say in what that blueprint looks like. By doing the work of opening up your funnel to allow for more and more intentions to make their way into your life, you are freeing yourself from the resistance of limiting beliefs.

The reality is that once you connect to the outcome with gratitude—or even just call in the feelings as we discussed earlier—it can show up immediately for you in your world.

The speed/likelihood with which any intention shows up, however, is filtered by two things:

1. Whether or not you believe it to be possible
2. The manner in which you believe it to be possible.

Just as we teach our students to take intentions into the silence to clean them of ego, we use silence to create space to see just where we are.

Listening as a state of being is essentially thinking and feeling with awareness, allowing us to break free from the slavery of the thinking mind. In its full form, to listen is to be the observer, and we work on this with our clients to bring it into their everyday experience.

To facilitate being in the receiving mode—getting out of your own way long enough to allow the thing you desire to be created—take a moment to pay attention to your internal dialogue and honestly ask yourself, *Am I in line with this event or outcome showing up in my life?*

Often, it is merely a matter of getting rid of the gremlins of doubt, and we work with several tools to push the gremlins out and start microshifting into the receiving mode. Gremlins, or the monkey mind, are a very common experience for many people. There is really no need to beat yourself up for having them, nor to think that all is hopeless just because you do! If you are stuck, then I again extend the offer to speak to a member of my team. Creating strategies that empower people to shake loose from these gremlins is a big part of what we do so well.

By now, you have:

Owned your creative power.

Become present.

Connected to the outcome by feeling gratitude for it in advance.

Now, it's time to check in and see where the resistance is, all the while ensuring that you are ready to take the actions and make the choices that honor your belief systems.

Celebrations… and Why We Celebrate

Over at www.dreamwithdan.com, we refer to celebrations as:

> **'Honoring your creation with an activity that makes you feel good, whilst consciously connecting the experience to what you have achieved.'**

Celebration, the effective final piece of the creation puzzle, is often overlooked, and yet it is such a powerful tool to build the momentum leading to completely new states of being.

People always ask me, "How should I celebrate?"

Again, there is no cookie-cutter answer since it's highly personalized and individual. In short, a celebration is all about doing whatever makes *you* feel good, whilst consciously associating that you are enjoying this activity *because* of the outcome you have now witnessed.

Thus, no one can tell you that this or that celebration is the best one to engage in—it's all down to your own choice.

The bottom line is that gratitude is where the connection to creation happens. So when we hold the frequency and your creation shows up, celebrate in some way that has meaning for you!

Do you need some examples of celebration? Remember that I can't tell you what makes *your* heart sing, which is the cornerstone behind how celebration works—but I will, however, share some examples so that you can get some direction on where to look in your own life.

Some time ago, I had a call to put together a strategy for someone. One of her celebrations was going to her favorite coffee shop, getting a decadent cake, and people-watching for an hour or two with her phone turned off. That was what made her feel good! She felt she deserved that indulgent time out.

Another client purchased a driving experience for the day and drove a Formula One race car to celebrate an especially big win.

Another just wanted to get to a yoga class, something that had been denied her because of her busy schedule as a top-level entrepreneur.

Celebration in some form is important because your thoughts and feelings have chemicals and hormones associated with them that show up in your body. While I'm not a scientist, I do know that when you celebrate, and I mean truly celebrate, a plethora of empowering chemicals and hormones are produced in your body—ones that will give you a psychological and physical boost to hit the next goal, and the next. It delivers the best possible—and healthy—high! You already know that feeling of being on cloud nine after a major achievement of some kind—well, that comes from these amazing chemicals.

By celebrating, therefore, you effectively invite your body to produce more of these positive chemicals and hormones on command. And the fantastic news is that there's no end to the supply. Just keep on aiming and striving, and keep on having the wins—however big or small—and you will have more and more such moments.

These chemicals and hormones feel so good that you will crave them more and more. And that's a very good thing.

Allowing the mind to witness that a pleasant experience stands on the other side of action in the form of the chemicals and hormones released when you celebrate, invites it to conspire with you to produce more. Yes, the body and mind crave their 'fix'!

Through celebration, you invite your mind to support you in your choices as a new default setting. This means you will be supported in making choices or taking actions that support the production of these positive chemicals, as opposed to disempowering choices and actions that produce hormones associated with, for example, stress and anxiety.

When you celebrate your wins consciously, consistently, and deliberately, you connect your win to the experience of what you're celebrating. That cognitive connection gradually forms new patterns of experience and new patterns of expectation of the win. Now, when you move into our future creations in your mind and come up against the same resistance as earlier, you don't have the same resistance in belief— because the mind has something tangible to look to as evidence of you actually being a winner. Last time, it really worked out—and so can it again and again.

That evidence is now anchored into your experience of having luck, abundance, joy, and so on.

The bottom line is, you should celebrate the way that makes you feel best. The more you do, the more you'll see new patterns of success show up in your life.

Stacking and Staying Present to Your Creation

Step Four of the Beyond Intention paradigm is all about creating a space where you allow what you've created to show up for you.

Also, one thing that we don't often talk about is that you can actually undo your creation, and we will look at this too.

By now, you will have done a lot of work clearing out the mental garbage and junk that's been holding you back. From personal experience, I can share with you that keeping your mind in check is a big deal, so allow me to share my experience with stacking.

Stacking is a super powerful way to use clearing tools to microshift out of your most stuck states. I personally use this whenever anxiety tries to kick in, or when the depression wants to take over.

Stacking is the act of layering clearing tools on top of each other as a series of microshifts, a powerful way to break free of deep stuck states, especially those really dark spaces we sometimes find ourselves in where it looks like there is no way out.

Whenever I share the story about the time I hid from the world under my bed covers and didn't get out of bed for a couple of days, people often wrongly assume this was years ago. It wasn't. In fact, it was early 2016. I had not yet met Dr. Joe Dispenza, the teacher whose work would awake me to my mission on Earth. Meditation had been one of the practices I hadn't yet understood, and the main stumbling block that hampered my progress through the mystery schools.

This particular drop into the shadows bore a gift, however, as I ended up consciously taking myself through the stacking process. Since then, I have been able to apply this tool to different aspects of my life, as well as using it to support my clients.

Whilst in the throes of one of life's many storms, the light at the end of the tunnel often seems way too far in the distance to add any meaning. When this is the case, there is always a microshift you can make.

The good news is the process is simple. Ask yourself what tiny movement you can make in the direction of the end goal right in this very moment. Celebrate the step being taken and repeat the process until you are where you want to be. It may be that you need a break for a few minutes, hours, or even a day before you are ready to move ahead. But just keep going.

For me, stacking out of the pit of depression can look like the following process:

1. Pulling back the covers.
2. Breathing more deeply to activate my parasympathetic nervous system.
3. Sitting up.
4. Getting my feet on the floor and staying there for a while until I can get some music on that changes my mood.
5. Getting the blood flowing by moving my body or knocking out some push-ups.
6. Getting in the shower...and maybe from there, even going back to bed. Perhaps I work from bed that day while setting a baseline for getting a little farther from my bed the next day. Sometimes, I can get my clothes on after the shower and get far as the kitchen to have some food. Sometimes, there is no eating, and that's ok too.

Since meditation, heart coherence, and Kundalini yoga have become an integral part of my life, these powerful tools help me shift my state at lightning speed, and so the stack is a lot faster in generating results. This is my own experience, though, and the result of years of working on myself. I really don't want you to start holding yourself to a standard beyond the edge of your work. But know that if a mess like myself—one who was drowning in suicidal depression—can win at life, then so can you.

Even if you're just fifteen, you have spent fifteen years creating the state of being that comprises who you are today. Rewriting that program may take time, which is why it is so important to be gentle with yourself. Despite the fact that you may have some high-level impact tools like rapid transformation therapy, Neuro-Linguistic Programming, or hypnotherapy, unless you've completely rewritten the entire program all the way from your conception, to birth, to who you are today, there will always be the possibility of you slipping back into old patterns.

The only way to catch those rogue thoughts is to listen and be aware of them. Just know that listening is not a passive process. It's work because you have to be aware of the choices that you're making and the excuses that you're giving yourself, and then go back through this paradigm and clear them. Do this while accepting that you've created all that you are experiencing now, and accepting that you have the responsibility for creating something new.

Depending on what year you're reading this, I created this paradigm more than eleven years ago, and yet I still face limiting beliefs and continue to learn and grow each day.

One of the most important things I've learned about consciousness from some of the world's greatest teachers and thought leaders is that anyone who claims perfection while still embodied in this three-dimensional realm is a bloody liar. Those who have broken free of the confines of this level of conscious-ness no longer reside here. That is more of a conversa-tion for those in our school of Alchemic Life Creation, but I wanted to take a moment to tell you that you do not need to get caught up in the idea of perfection as a state of no longer needing to do the work. Love the work and do not pray for it to end. If you are not grow-ing, then you are dying.

Remember that up until now, as much as 95% of your life has been running on unconscious programs prob-ably not in your best interests.

According to my teacher Dr. Joe Dispenza, the brain has up to 60,000 to 90,000 daily thoughts. That's a lot of action being taken on your behalf, much of which may not even be for your highest or greatest good. When bumps in the road happen, relax, journal about them, and make a conscious decision to be aware of them next time.

Always remember the present moment is a reset button that's yours to enjoy on a moment-to-moment basis, so take advantage of it. If you falter, don't beat yourself up. Just make a new choice next time. In our Beyond Intention programs, we frame this in a concept entitled, 'You are your own best agent.' This means the person best suited to look out for your interests is the conscious part of you, the part that made the deliberate decision to live a joyful life.

Creation, or we could say the connection to the creation, happens in Step Three: Gratitude, but more often than not, shows up in the silence of listening required in Step Four. Maxwell Maltz's book, *Psycho-Cybernetics*, teaches us that guided missiles actually get to their target by making adjustments whenever they veer off course. We're going to do that same thing by building a relationship with your inner voice, the individual guidance system that lets you know when you're off course. With that feedback in hand, you can then start making decisions from a state of power.

A thought from the author:

'God did not make things complicated; man did, so who's to say that it's impossible?'

I quote myself here to highlight an important point— that this is not a complicated process.

How should you listen? There are plenty of tools to choose from, and much like the clearing toolkit, it's just a matter of building a personal relationship with what works for you.

Consider journaling, taking time to get in touch with your instincts, intuition, and gut feelings, getting comfortable with and spending time in silence, meditation, Tai Chi, Yoga, and other forms of meditative practice.

For some people, it's going for a run or spending some time in nature. Some of our clients love to dance. Personally, I deeply connect to my inner guidance when playing the piano.

My journey into daily meditation has not only been supercharged by self-awareness, but it has also elevated me into the seat of being the observer of my thoughts, enabling me to fully observe them from a space of peaceful silence. As a result, meditation now forms an integral part of our workshops and retreats, and has become *the* go-to tool for our clients and students.

Through this tool, we enable and empower our students to build capacity and propensity to listen deeply to the song of their soul—the most beautiful and powerful part of each person.

With that said, I'd like *you* to pick a few tools to better help you begin listening. Choose from the examples above that best serve you, then start journaling about your journey into listening.

Dreaming with Your Eyes Open

In my second book, *The Dreamer's Manifesto*, I spoke at length about the meaning of my slogan, "Dream with Your Eyes Open." Beyond Intention's place in the landscape of my overall mission is to provide a tool to support you. Using this tool, you can make choices that empower you to create your dream.

The *Dreamer's Manifesto* invited you to see that you are worth so much more than you have allowed yourself to be. Beyond Intention, on the other hand, guides you to not only make this truth a tangible goal you can experience, but it also gives you the tools to do so with grace, ease, and flow.

As I say in what is perhaps my favorite keynote talk, there is a pointlessness to purpose when not accompanied by action. Beyond Intention provides the tools to create a container for purpose-driven action, yielding results on command.

While I will not use the word *enlightenment,* once you fully integrate the Beyond Intention paradigm into your life, you will find that many of the problems, challenges, people, places, and things previously forming your emotional baggage—things that have been holding you back—are really a whole lot of nothing.

Once you begin living and embodying Beyond Intention, you will begin to think and feel with a new awareness. To achieve this state of being, you need to fully integrate the demands of this paradigm. As you become more in tune with the underlying thoughts and feelings that have been running your life, the natural progression from this state of being is that you begin seeing *all* of these things for what they really are. More importantly, you start to see yourself for who you really are.

In marrying the message of *The Dreamer's Manifesto* and this book, consider for a moment what life would be like if the only intention you had was to know your purpose for being on this Earth, and to embody and live your contribution to the world.

While this didn't happen overnight, I came to the point in my life where I stopped chasing after people, places, and things with my energy and intentions.

Instead, the one place where I focused my energy in terms of manifesting and creating was in a day-to-day existence where I enjoyed the honor of sharing my unique gifts with the world. In doing so, I began living my true purpose.

For me, that's represented by my mission statement:

"Spearhead an evolutionary uplift in universal consciousness by awakening people to the importance of their Unique Role already encoded within. This deep and often ignored or undervalued passion is defined as their Dream."

I now no longer have individual, self-directed intentions of any kind—well, for the most part at least. Every morning as part of my daily routine, I re-center myself and set my intention toward one thing—living my purpose. I use a tool called a Macro Intention to anchor this in, reverting to that anchor multiple times throughout my day.

In the *Dreamer's Manifesto*, I also speak at length about the importance of not letting other people dictate what you should and should not deem as part of your dream. To that end, I'm not saying that you cannot have intentions centered on people, places, and things. The choice is always yours.

What I am sharing with you is an invitation to see just how beautiful life can be if your intention is singular and in line with your purpose.

By now, I'm sure you know the tools I've shared with you in this book are designed to help you create the life you want—free from the limitations of the past—with a focus on building the future of your own design.

Ultimately, what I'm asking you to do is remain open to the possibility that the future you are in the process of creating is going to be so much better than you could have imagined—and when it shows up, it will come in a way you never could have envisaged.

CLOSING THOUGHTS

I want to thank and celebrate you for stepping up and giving this type of creation a try. So many people go through their lives as slaves to their circumstances.

By choosing to take a meaningful stake in the game, you are opening yourself up to a world of possibilities where anything you welcome and truly believe in can become a reflection of what you experience.

I would like to leave you with some closing thoughts regarding setting and experiencing intended outcomes:

1. Own that *you* are the only one responsible for creating the outcome of your intention. Denying this ownership only gives your power away, or in other words, the responsibility is still on you.

2. Get clear on the feelings associated with your intention.

3. Own the stories that stand in your way, and know that they do not have to stay.

4. Microshift your energy into the alignment of your mindset and actions with your intention.

5. Celebrate every win along the way and every movement in the right direction.

Do this, and you will always create your outcomes, live Beyond Intention, and realize that a way of being is available to you that doesn't even require you to set intentions anymore.

Until that day, however, have fun and remember that there is an infinite amount of joy available to you if you're ready to make a choice to enjoy life.

Remember that everything you seek is already here and now, and that you are not even really creating anything so much as setting intentions in the now. It all starts with clearing your life of the resistance that keeps your intention from making its way from the pure energy of the 5th Dimension, all the way to the matter you experience with your senses in this three-dimensional reality.

Keep dreaming with your eyes open.

D.

WHAT COMES NEXT?

The most important thing for you to do now is to implement this work into your life, honor the importance of microshifting, and begin the work of populating your life—one step at a time—with the principles we have explored.

There are plenty of free resources on my website, www.DreamWithDan.com, as well as a host of free content on my YouTube, Facebook, and Instagram channels to help and guide you. All links are on my website, but you can also find them below:

Instagram: @dreamerceo
Twitter: @dreamerceo
Clubhouse: @dreamerceo
Facebook page: @thedreamerceo
Facebook Group: www.dreamwithdan.com/facebook
LinkedIn:
www.dreamwithdan.com/linkedin
YouTube:

www.doitwithdan.tv
Everyone has a different learning style. Some
prefer groups, others one-on-one attention.
To further your education, and/or if you feel
you need an accountability partner,
consider the following:

Free Strategy Calls

Via a free, no-obligation strategy call, my team and I
are waiting to support you in employing the tools pre-
sented in this book.

Online Programs and Beyond Intention University

We also have a very powerful collection of online programs with access starting from as little as $47 per
month, and as I write this, our membership program
to Beyond Intention University is still on a special offer
priced at less than a monthly coffee budget.

Membership gives you access to group coaching calls,
led personally by me, as well as a series of classes held
by members of my coaching team.

You also gain access to special guests covering a wide
range of areas including, but not limited to, health,
relationships, and financial abundance.

Also included in membership is access to the different
levels of valuable information in our online programs.

All core online programs are available at our most basic level, with other available levels offering more hands-on support, as well as access to all live streams and online events. And all levels gain access to our exclusive, paid, online community.

Podcast

In addition, there are my 'Do it with Dan' podcast and 'Beyond Success' podcasts are available on all major platforms.

Online Programs

You can, of course, gain access to any of our individual online programs without becoming a member of Beyond Intention University. The next step in the order of our core suggested syllabus would be the Beyond Intention Basics. This is if you really want to dig deeper into the paradigm—or you can advance to the Create Your Ideal Life program. All of these are available on my website: www.dreamwithdan.com.

One-on-One Coaching

If you would like to take the step of discussing one-on-one coaching with one of my team, then go ahead and schedule an Eyes Open Deep Dive via www.dreamwith-dan.com/dive. Not everyone is ready to be coached, and even for those who are ready to be coached, the Beyond Intention model may not be right for you.

For many people, coaching represents the opportunity to apportion blame for the inevitable result of you not doing the work that your subconscious never planned to do anyway. We have strict protocols in place for this and screen our clients to ensure that they are 100% committed to the process.

Dream Beyond Intention Mastermind

If you are still seeking something more than just coaching, another option might be the Dream Beyond Intention Mastermind. This level of working with us is designed to completely overhaul your life and support you in reconstructing every element of it. We do this by developing a blueprint we spend twelve months together writing and executing. This is the only level of working with us that includes working directly with me.

The Dream Beyond Intention Mastermind also includes access to up to three private VIP deep-dive weekends with just me and your fellow Mastermind Members. Numbers are limited. It includes a host of other benefits aligned with our teaching that entitle you to an abundant life, including a personal lifestyle concierge and access to a private jet account.

Also included at this level is free access to any of the workshops offered around the globe, and deep-discounted access to Beyond Intention retreats.

I have a dozen world-class thought leaders and teachers supporting this Mastermind, which also includes lifetime access to every program we create, including non-core syllabus programs such as Micro2Millions 2.0.

Case Studies & Testimonials

Please note that all names used here have been changed to protect clients' privacy. Thank you all for trusting me to be a part of your expansion, and I Love You.

<u>Family Life and Purpose – Meet Sammy</u>

Sammy's story comprises one my favorite types of case study. He was not in a program, nor did he do any formal coaching with me or the team. He simply demonstrates what is possible when someone is truly ready to step into the work, having only gotten a recording of a Beyond Intention Foundations workshop.

> "Since listening to the Beyond Intention workshop earlier this year, I felt like Dan was talking directly to me. I remember listening to it in the gym and having to stop my workout, pick up my shit and sit down and start from the beginning. I sat there for over two hours and soaked it in and realised that I'd been doing everything my other motivational

speakers had been suggesting but Dan brought the most important rule, which to me is acceptance.

That, coupled with the common denominator paradigm, meant I was hit like a train by this way of thinking. And although my life wasn't bad and I was making progress in many areas, that workshop held up a huge mirror and opened me up to some things I had tried to bury deep down.

It made me realise I wasn't living the life I wanted, wasn't working toward the way I should have been, and that shit needed to change—and it wasn't outside of myself.

I built one day at a time, not being too hard on myself and creating the life I wanted through new behaviours, meditation, and the right mental environment including the people I surrounded myself with.

I want to thank Dan from way down deep for packaging this, alongside the podcasts, in a digestible, simple easy to follow way. The only way I can put this is that I've levelled up and taken total control of my life. I've jumped out the back seat, taken the wheel and really believe that I am making the changes I've always wanted but only halfheartedly pushed for in the past.

My marriage is improving daily and I've faced some big fears (like jumping out of a plane at 15,000 feet). I am becoming a better father, person and made some big life decisions which are bearing fruit now with my new perspective—and the micro-shifts I've learnt from this guy are real game changers!

I can't thank him enough for giving me the extra tools and confidence I so desperately needed to improve my life and those around me."

Love and Relationships – Meet Marie

I had the pleasure of working with Marie one on one. Marie had been experiencing, as she saw it, that every man she was attracting was unavailable by distance or ended up already being in relationship. She was sick and tired of this pattern showing up in her life and wanted a change as this had been playing out time and time again for almost two years.

Marie's situation was one of those instances where it took me less than twenty minutes to identify the root problem, and using Beyond Intention-based protocols, provide her with tools that led to a most magical result. Less than twelve months later, and Marie is now engaged to the love of her life.

Freedom from the Rat Race – Meet Amanda

Amanda is a caregiver who sought to build her business so that she could have more time in her day to meet those duties in a relaxed way.

This would just not be possible in a traditional 9-5 job and so Amanda sought support in building up her own business via Beyond Success and Micro2Millions.

Amanda learned to focus, not only on taking action, but also on being aligned energetically with what she wanted, and with exactly how to create what she desired. She learned to move step by step in flow, in the face of real-world challenges. Of course, she also needed revenue, having stepped out in faith and left a job that no longer served her. Amanda literally had no money to pay the bills.

Amanda now has a number of paid group classes and is leveraging those to build out additional business where she serves private clients. Working with us, she also has access to an extended community where she gets leads and opportunities to share her work with thousands of people all over the globe.

For Amanda though, she is just much happier and more relaxed, no longer tied to a job she didn't like and she has something precious that money cannot directly buy—more time for her day-to-day caregiving activities.

<u>Belief in the Human Spirit – Meet Kingsley</u>

Kingsley didn't think people cared as much as they do. Having started a non-profit with family members and some friends, this lack of belief in others led to him stopping asking as many people to donate to the charity.

Kingsley learned all about the Money Game – a free resource available at www.DreamWithDan.com as part of the Micro2Millions online program, and through this expanded his beliefs around not only money, but people too! The Money Game is a Beyond Intention-powered tool that supports you in creating internal alignment with your intentions, and teaches you how to do this through the playful manifesting of money.

Not only did he let go of his fears and start talking to people about supporting his charitable works from a place of expansion and abundance, but he also started having more fun during these interactions. He says that the energy shifts could be felt not only by him, but also the people he was engaging with.

I love working with people like Kingsley who genuinely want to go out and do good in the world.

Beyond Intention in the Corporate World – Meet Karen

Karen did not know what she wanted to express her gratitude for, and so here is her own personal testimonial about her experience with Beyond Intention and private coaching with me.

Karen works in top-flight finance and applies her doctorate to structuring finance deals as large as nine figures in the pharmaceutical world. It was and continues to be my absolute pleasure to support her expansion.

> "I had a lack of clarity and self-confidence about what I felt I was here to do. I had a murky idea, or rather a set of jumbled ideas and intuitions, but no clear picture. Dan's questions, listening, frameworks and extreme clarity pulled me along a thread that was there but seemed to be invisible to me, while in clear sight to Dan. He helped me discover for myself, by skillful prodding and strategic questioning, what it is that I aim to create, and he then proceeded to instill in me the confidence that *of course, I could do it, one micro step at a time*. He made it so obvious, and it suddenly seemed easy.
>
> I didn't know how to get started or what to do. After speaking with Dan and clarifying what it was that I was after, and how I could

get started doing it, it was as if my seeing of the problem—huge, as I didn't know where to start and what to do—shifted to manageable, with clear first steps, and then next steps, goals, and clarity about the vision and starting path.

I started seeing much more clearly what I was doing and why. From that, I started believing it was not that hard, was worthwhile, and entirely possible. From there, and with Dan's help, the first steps now felt kind of obvious—and my whole relationship to the project that I had seen as a problem radically shifted. I felt much more empowered, greatly supported, and far clearer.

Dan instilled in me the belief that I really could do this, that I absolutely had something valuable to share.

I feel much more certain in my ability to create what I wish to create, and the value of doing it. His skillful questioning, and poking at my disempowering stories, plus great humor, really helped me out of excessive seriousness.

His teaching about the value of micro steps and celebrating little wins changed my approach, and helped me to get started. Turns out when

I did, the project started moving faster and with more ease than I had anticipated.

Dan also kept me honest when I would get into disempowering states by just offering an immediate alternative way to see the situation, and he did it with such skill and compassion, it was impossible not to shift to a more empowered state.

I have felt deeply supported and held when working with Dan, for in his energy, somehow, more is possible than on my own or with most other professionals who may bring skills, but may not have his unique and powerful presence. His gift is exceptional, and his humanity, love and compassion for what he does and who he does it with and for, are all extraordinary.

I sometimes think *what would Dan say or do,* when faced with a question. I may not call him, but even just contemplating that can bring clarity and ease."

Giving Marriage a Second Chance – Meet Marcus

Marcus was on the verge of losing his marriage since unbeknownst to him at the time of attending my event, his wife was only holding out for him to get on his feet before serving divorce papers. A car accident had thrown his life off track and he was in a downward spiral, heading nowhere great.

He was a very interesting participant in the master-mind event, asking poignant questions and, as someone completely new to my work that day, working with a blank slate regarding his expectations.

That blank slate, however, represented a complete 180-degree flip by the time Marcus returned home that day.

Not only did he tearfully mend the wounds with his wife and create space for a second chance, but he also reached out to his estranged father to begin work on that relationship too.

Marcus also worked on an advanced Ideal Life Blueprint that day, and has been microshifting into existence with the full support of his loved ones, manifesting a lovingly abundant life that he now knows he deserves and is worthy of having.

Getting Down to Business – Meet Joy

Joy was one of the attendees at our retreat on the idyllic island of Malta. As a business owner, she has a lot of pressures that she juggles daily, so I was honoured that she took the time out to spend with us on the retreat:

"The Malta Retreat was epic! Dan had several one-on-one coaching calls with me, to get me ready to develop my ideal life blueprint on the trip!

While there, it was the perfect mix of camaraderie and learning.

Dan is a true gift to this world. His unique style of getting to the center of what I want to create in my life was truly amazing.

The retreat catapulted me into the next right steps for me and my business. If you get the chance to go on a retreat with Dan, do it! You will never look back!"

Permission for Playful Purpose – Meet Rene

Before Rene attended a Beyond Intention Retreat, she was stuck in life. Not only was she unsure about what she describes as her 'purpose, direction and reasons", but she was also feeling disconnected and scared to take any first steps.

She was drowning in unworthiness and a helpless feeling of not doing what she wanted with her life. She explained to me that she was *Feeling stupid for not committing to the things I want to do. Out of flow. Feeling stuck.*

After the time we spent together, Rene felt connected again to a sense of purpose and tapped back into feeling worthy, present and free. She reported feeling fun again and that she had been given permission to create her best life. She realised that she deserved it and gained a sense of meaning in relation to herself and her environment.

"I have a lot to offer to me and the world, feel fun and look forward to applying my new knowledge and feelings in my everyday life!

I am unique. I have a lot to offer as a coach and therapist. Have a lot of knowledge to bring into this world, to connect and guide people in the connection with themselves.

Overall, I feel more gratitude and blessed to be alive. I have something to do in this world. And while doing it, I have as much fun as possible. I can create an easy life, deserve that, and feel confident.

Dan's quote, 'first you have to be in service to be of service' really is present in me. New focus. Practice and play. Creating is fun.

Not going to lie and tell you everything that was holding me back magically disappeared.

But I have easy, fun and practical tools now to really make that change. I realise and accept I sometimes make hedges or illusions. I can see them and give them the love and light they need, or snap out of it, without judging.

With acceptance, I can go to the feeling I need to feel about my intention."

From Trauma to Self-Love – Meet Ruth

Ruth experienced my work for the first time at a Beyond Intention retreat. Following the trauma of a stillbirth, she had given up living for herself and had moved abroad to be the full-time carer for her grand-parents, and yet had only touched her early thirties.

Ruth stated at the start of the retreat that she was saddened by never having had a career or purpose of her own; it was clear that the thread for her was worthiness, and living under the thumb of other people's expectations of what she should want for her life.

I'll let Ruth tell you the rest of her story:

"I've always plodded through life not really feeling worthy enough to make my own choices. I've hidden behind other people's needs and desires. I never knew what I wanted to be doing, because I was clouded by illusions and stories of what others were saying I should be doing.

Dan helped open my eyes to my own worth. Everyone has heard 'you can't pour from an empty cup', but how about thinking what we're filling that cup with?

I'm already more proactive and motivated for me, not solely to think about other people's lives but to think about mine. I've never lived so much in the present or felt so focused. Something that really resonated with me was how we live in trauma from the past, or anxious for the future, whereas all we need to be is *present in our present.*

I don't feel the need to think about family or friends before I've even decided what I need to get done in a day. I feel lighter, more positive and more proactive already.

I'm currently researching a month-long yoga retreat to do just for myself. This will help qualify me to teach more types of yoga all over the world. This will provide me with the financial freedom and independence I deserve and will enable me to travel and enjoy the world.

I no longer feel the need to stay and live other people's lives.

Dan the man! I can't recommend him enough. Love, love, love him."

Owning a Desire for the Abundant Life – Meet Wayne

Wayne joined Beyond Intention University as a bonus for signing up to the Micro2Millions program and is also joining me for a retreat in Cabo, Mexico. I look forward to updating this case study in a later edition of this book.

Wayne was looking for inspiration, and wanted to start connecting with people internationally who were looking for the same expansion in their lives as he was. He felt that he was limited by his network, and because of that, expansion possibilities seemed limited.

He found this connection in our community, and now is forming bonds with just the caliber of person he desired, as well as now enjoying expansion into a quantum reality of infinite possibilities.

Wayne is owning his desires for more life now, and has opened up to his power to choose the experiences he has in his life. He also sets his intention daily, and in his own words:

> "Every day, I wake up and set my intentions. Good things happen! What enjoyment/ uplift/expansion has come in? My life is very hopeful! Perhaps an inconvenience has dissipated?"

Self-love, Personal Power and the Man of Her Dreams – Meet Jacqueline

Hear from entrepreneur Jacqueline who tells in her own words how private Beyond Intention coaching completely shifted her experience – even though at first, she had some resistance to my way of working…

> "I started coaching with Dan in a period when I was still going though grieving from my past relationship. I had low self-confidence and I didn't know what I want to do my life. I'd closed my business a year before that. I came to Dan hoping that he could help me find my propose in life again.
>
> I wasn't very fulfilled, and was blaming myself. I felt I couldn't trust myself and what I wanted in life; I always had to ask permission.
>
> I really enjoyed working with Dan. I actually knew Dan for a while before I decided to coach with him. I always loved his energy; he is vibrating at very high frequency, and he has a very kind heart and is someone who has a lot of compassion, so I feel I can open up to him. It's not easy for me to open up to a male coach.
>
> In our coaching relationship, he really helped me see my blind spots, how everything is

connected and is never a surface thing. For example, when I went travelling with a group of people and I was really struggling with them, as I didn't really get on with them.

I was making myself unhappy and was very sad and confused with what was going on. Dan helped me to see that I don't really honour myself and my needs; it was actually connecting to my self-love!

With his works about setting up intentions and microshifts in the beginning, I didn't really resonate with him. I was like, *I don't want to make a small step!* I am the kind of person who wants to make big steps, so there was some resistance; however, after working with him for a while and applying his method, I started to see why this was a way that worked for me, because it was really about setting myself up to win."

Jacqueline has since got back in the saddle not only with business, but with love, and is now engaged to the love of her life:

"Dan has really helped me in this process of trusting myself and speaking up for what I want in life, so I was able to attract the man I wanted!

I set up an intention every day that I want to work on, and for the feelings I want. :)"

Join me in celebrating Jacqueline...

I have a folder full of testimonials and case studies of people from all walks of life and with all forms of challenges.

Who is Daniel Mangena?

After receiving a late diagnosis of Asperger's and experiencing life-shattering trauma at age twenty, Daniel spent seven years struggling to keep the effects of these events from spilling into every aspect of his life.

Daniel initially developed Beyond Intention as a lifeline while he grappled with suicidal thoughts and ideation, and soon found this simple, four-step process transformed his life from misery to celebration. Daniel realized he could help others do the same, and thus Beyond Intention was born.

Daniel discovered a path to lasting joy and purpose in his life, and wants nothing more than to share with others the tools that saved his life. To that end, he lives by this mission statement:

"Spearhead an evolutionary uplift in universal consciousness by awakening people to the importance of their Unique Role already encoded within. This deep and often ignored or undervalued passion is defined as their Dream."

Daniel shares his vision of empowerment and joy globally via public speaking, workshops, books he has authored, blogging, and his Do it with Dan podcast series. In addition, Daniel offers individual and group coaching and consultations.

Daniel is also a voracious reader and publicly documents his challenge to read a book every week. He loves to travel, write, perform as a singer-songwriter, practice Kundalini yoga, meditation, and stays active with Brazilian Jiu-jitsu. He is an outspoken promoter of entrepreneurial philanthropy, and an ambassador for the Mangena Foundation. He works with several charities across the globe and is a patron of many.

To contact Daniel, visit www.dreamwithdan.com. He can also be found on most major social media platforms with the handle @dreamerCEO.

Booking Daniel to Speak

Dynamic, insightful and inspirational, Daniel is available to deliver keynote talks and presentations globally.

Feel free to contact the team to explore Daniel facilitating a Beyond Intention workshop in your area, as well as to guest teach at your workshop or retreat.

Bring the power of Beyond Intention to your event and consider taking your business or workplace to the next level with Daniel's unique and exclusive tools.

Corporate training is also available via <u>www.dreamwithdan.com.</u>

Daniel also loves the opportunity to speak to and work with educators and student audiences. Talks and training can be tailored to your individual intentions, and you are invited to book a no-obligation, free consultation to ensure that optimal alignment is created for an expansive outcome.

Clearing Tools Encyclopedia

This encyclopedia is by no means exhaustive and represents just a snapshot into the world of clearing. Some recommended reading for further tools is The Key by Joe Vitale, a book that we gift to all of our private coaching clients.

Clearing, as you know by now, is about getting present and back to love. This is a personal process and so you must compile your own personal clearing toolbox with knowledge and understanding of you in mind.

Play with this list, using the principles to identify further options and journal your adventure.

Again, this list is by no means exhaustive and remember that a combination of tools may be required for different stuck states and energy traps.

Mind Your Language

Speak in absolutes and not possibilities — use *I will* or *I am* and lose the *might,* the *possibly,* the *hopefully* and the *someday*—and most definitely the *can't.*

Lose *try to* and *hope to,* and *think about doing*, and all these words loaded with disempowerment and with the potential for failure.

As soon as you say you *will try to do* something, or *will hopefully achieve* it, or *might give it a go sometime*— you're opening the possibility for *not* doing it and, ultimately, for failing.

Say no to all those *might-do's.*

You *will* do it.

You *are doing it*.

That's the whole story. Your story.

Binaural Frequencies & Healing Music

Stream tapestries of music composed in 432Hz and 444Hz stitched with binaural & isochronic solfeggio tones, nature sounds, bells, chimes, and crystal bowls. By listening to audio reproductions of harmonious brainwave states and carefully crafted compositions in alternate tunings, music is able to harmonize your mood, mind, body, office and living spaces.

Your mind exists in five different brainwave states throughout the day depending on your activity, and also corresponding to your emotions and mood. If you're tired midday and wish to perk up, you need to bring your brainwave state from theta to alpha, beta, or gamma.

If you're wired and frazzled and would like to focus, then you need to balance the hemispheres of your brain and bring your mind into a balanced theta, alpha, or beta state.

By listening to audio reproductions of a desired brainwave state, you can put yourself into your desired corresponding mood state within minutes.

Live with your heart forward and your mind open. Peace & Love.

Learn more at Sinesmusic.com & Gregpapania.com

Option Method
- Bruce Di Marsico
This explanation of The Option Method is taken from www.optionmethodnetwork.com and is written by Deborah Mendal.

We are all on a constant quest for happiness. We are searching in our own personal ways. Some of us are looking for that perfect relationship with a loved one or the satisfying career. Or maybe it's a house in the country with a family that we want, or perhaps we are grasping for that seemingly unattainable spiritual center. Whatever our desires, we usually look outside ourselves for help to attain them.

In varying degrees, we feel that we need something more than what we already possess spiritually or materialistically before we can be really happy. Some of us get closer to it than others. Often, a life-threatening illness or the profound loss of a loved one becomes a turning point in our lives, a pivotal moment, when we make a conscious choice to be grateful for what we have and live life to the fullest.

For some, as the routines of life return, this awakening remains in the heart and soul, like a gift from God, but it slips from the grasp of others. How can we hold onto happiness in all its forms: contentment, joy, gratitude, peacefulness, bliss?

How might we live a life feeling good about ourselves, knowing that we feel exactly how we want to feel, that nothing can make us feel a way that we don't want to feel, and that we already are equipped with everything we need to achieve happiness?

We don't *need* a new mantra or affirmation, teacher, workshop, or guru to find our path. Although, once we've opened the door to our hearts, we may experience joy and growth with any one or more of them as we travel through life. I invite you now on a journey, your own personal expedition to discover personal wisdom and happiness.

To begin this journey, we must first start where we now are. To get in touch with ourselves, our true happiness and spirit, we must begin by removing the layers of beliefs that conceal it. This is an easy and painless process when we use the Option Method questions.

Sometimes, we experience ourselves as a living contradiction. We feel a way we don't want to feel. How is this possible and how can we end it?

The Option questions will help us to identify and to clarify, and thus expose to the light the current mistaken belief that's clouding our vision and obscuring the truth that already resides in our hearts. Once we begin this process, if we are honest with ourselves, we won't go back. It is in our very nature always to desire happiness. God gave each of us a soul which burns like an eternal flame with this desire to be happy. Sometimes, we let our happiness shine, when it's *appropriate* or when we feel *allowed.* At other times, it is obscured by our fears and hesitations. Depending on our currently held mistaken beliefs, we may simply just not feel right or may be in total despair.

Love it – Ho'oponopono (ho-o-pono-pono)
- Hawaiian practice of reconciliation and forgiveness.

'The Hawaiian word translates into English simply as *correction*, with the synonyms *manage* or *supervise*, and the antonym *careless*.[1][2] Similar forgiveness practices are performed on islands throughout the South Pacific, including Hawaii, Samoa, Tahiti and New Zealand. Traditional *Ho'oponopono* is practiced by indigenous Hawaiian healers, often within the extended family by a family member. There is also a New Age practice that goes by the same name.' Wikipedia

I learned all about this practice in Joe Vitale's book, Zero Limits. What is the basic principle in action? Look at anything that needs healing and send it constant and deliberate loving energy.

Have a Happy Song

Find a song that makes you want to shake your booty and play it whenever you get into a funk. When that song stops working, find another one!

Stop Complaining

Complaining is at its core really an exercise in attention seeking that serves no purpose other than locking the complaint in your reality vortex.

By continuing to complain, you lock yourself in the energy of the thing and keep your focus and attention on it.

In that space, there cannot be a shift away from it. And remember, complaining is the very opposite of gratitude.

Talk it out (and not in)

Therapy is a powerful tool when properly employed. Approach it from a state of empowerment, using it as an opportunity to explore what must be healed from a present State of Acceptance in a safe and supported space. Therapy is also a space to get the 'junk' off your chest; it is better out than in, but let it out to stay out, not for you to stay in (the energy of) the person, place or thing you are talking about.

Make Someone's Day

Take the opportunity to shift the energetic focus in your own life and do something good for someone else without the expectation of anything in return.

Micro-shift

Start small, with just one thing and do it now. Get up, dress up and do one small, achievable thing. Pick some low-hanging fruit that you can celebrate in the next five minutes and get into a new rhythm in a new direction that better serves you, and that moves away from your current stuck state.

Start your day with just one thing in focus: peace of mind. As you work through the paradigm, aim to address just one small thing for the day/week. This could be always say *thank you,* to say *I love you* to yourself in the mirror at least once per day—nothing too taxing, just enough to get moving.

Cut the Cord

When all else fails, there are times when extreme action is needed. In those instances, make a plan, line up the appropriate support, and:

- Leave the relationship or friendship
- Get a new job

- Move to a new physical space and change your environment – sometimes this may only need to be short term such as a sin bin or time out

- You are not doing this for the disempowered pursuit of putting your head in the sand or running away, but to create space to work on yourself.

Virtual Hugs

When your stuck state revolves around a person, try this exercise.

Close your eyes, take a deep breath and count to 3. Then release and hold the image of the number 3.

Take another deep breath, hold for three and release, holding a mental image of the number 2. Repeat a third time, now holding an image of you holding the person in the warmest embrace. Hold them in your mind's eye, keeping your breath deep and deliberate while focusing on your heart and remaining like this until the energy in the mental scene translates into a positive vibration.

It is important that you do all this in the first person, as in you are the one doing the holding. See the scene as yourself, with your own eyes, holding them with the mental extension of your arms. Repeat anytime in which thoughts of the person come up, combined with the feelings from which you want to shift.

This exercise can also be done with a past version of yourself. Hug a representation of yourself in a place where the energetic baggage holds, and keep on hugging until it is gone.

Meditation

In his book, Becoming Supernatural, Dr JD describes meditation as a *model to change our internal state.* By cutting attention to the outside world and the senses, you can allow space for separation from the baggage tying you energetically, mentally, or emotionally to your current life situation.

VIP Day

A neat trick I learned from Stuart Goldsmith in his book The Midas Method is to shift your energy by pampering yourself for the day. I use T Harv Eker's tool of the play jar to fund my VIP days and also tie this in to celebration (Beyond Intention Step 4).

Float

Spend time in a sensory deprivation tank. A lot of major cities now have these and they offer the opportunity to completely cut off from the world and have a hard reset.

Change Your Inputs

Stop reading the papers and watching the news, curating your social media feeds. Or even consider coming off social media for a while. I did it for twelve months and I'm still alive.

What TV shows are you watching? What book are you reading right now?

How are these things making you feel? Switch your sensory inputs to ones that serve your joy.

Change Your Physiology

Get up, move your body, smile, straighten your back and shake your booty – physiological changes have an effect on your mood.

Laugh

Identify the people, places and things that force you to smile and keep them available to you. This could be a friend whose jokes are so bad that you have to laugh, or a stand-up show by your favourite comedian. I have been known to go on YouTube and look for comedy clips or even check out memes on social media for this purpose.

Exercise

Running and other forms of exercise release endorphins into the blood stream. These are scientifically proven to give you the space to make new choices about your mood.

Breathing Exercises

A number of different types of breathing exercises can be explored to change your mood, increase your energy and even heal your body. I personally practice Kundalini yoga, but there are many tools like this that can shift you in a matter of minutes.

Reiki

This is a form of alternative medicine developed in 1922 by Mikao Usui.[1][2] Since originating in Japan, reiki has been adapted into varying cultural traditions across the world. Reiki practitioners use a technique called *palm healing* or *hands-on healing* through which a universal energy is said to be transferred through the palms of the practitioner to the patient, to encourage emotional or physical healing.

www.khrystlerea.com

RTT – Rapid Transformation Therapy
- Marisa Peer

Rapid Transformational Therapy embraces many of the positive aspects of hypnosis and hypnotherapy that are known to produce a transformative effect on clients:

the use of trance, regression, and hypnotic conditioning. However RTT goes beyond, diagnosing what works with clients to build a new therapeutic approach. Unlike many hypnotherapy approaches, RTT does not rely solely on positive reinforcement.

Make a Commitment and Stick to it

"If you make an agreement with yourself to be impeccable with your word, with just that intention, the truth will manifest through you and clean all the emotional poison that exists within you."

Don Miguel Ruiz, The Four Agreements.

EFT (Emotional Freedom Technique)

EFT or Tapping is a form of energy psychology in which you tap on meridian endpoints on the face and body while focusing on whatever issue you are working on.

EFT is wonderful for releasing trapped painful memories from the body, whether physical or emotional, as well as for releasing phobias, stress, sadness or anger, to name a few. These are just a few examples of the countless ways in which EFT can help you clear blocks or limiting beliefs that may hold you back from creating the life of your dreams.

Learn more at www.solace4me.com

Matrix Reimprinting
- Karl Dawson

An offshoot of EFT, 'Matrix Reimprinting' is another form of energy psychology in which you use EFT Tapping while going into the past to serve the younger self who is in need.

Think of it as looking at a past painful event as if it is happening in a play, and the current self goes back to help the younger self to be seen and heard, figuring out how to handle the situation in an empowering way. Matrix Reimprinting is absolutely amazing at shifting old perspectives and blocking beliefs into powerful, unstoppable thinking.

Learn more at YourTappingJourney.com

Matrix Birth Reimprinting (MBR)
-Sharon King

Created by Sharon King, Author of *Heal Your Birth, Heal Your Life,* Matrix Birth Reimprinting (MBR), uses the principles of Matrix Reimprinting and enables clients to go back and transform their preconscious experiences of being in utero and their own birth.

Perhaps one of the most impacting traumas that a baby can experience is birth. It's not that birth itself has to be a traumatic experience. It's that our Western birthing process has become highly mechanical. This is largely because it has not been understood that babies are conscious beings. With the misunderstanding that babies can't feel or remember anything, they are often brought into the world in barbaric ways with forceps, needles and rough handling, as well as overlooking the vital opportunity they need to bond with their mother as nature intended.

The minute a baby experiences this kind of treatment, it makes a decision about the world it lives in—a decision it often carries for the rest of its life.

The MBR process can also be used to help mothers transform the traumas of giving birth previously and to enable mothers-to-be to achieve a peaceful and natural birth. Perhaps one of the most surprising revelations has come from the fact that rewriting a birth of a child, through the mother, can have an effect on their current child's health and wellbeing.

Other benefits of MBR include working with infertility, loss of a child, and adoption.

For more information go to www.magicalnewbeginnings.com and www.healyourbirthbook.com

ALL Formula
- Pernilla Lilarose

Most of us spend a great deal of time resisting what we don't want in life, not realizing that this resistance is what keeps us out of the Divine Flow and painfully stuck in what we don't want.

The ALL Formula, Allow – Listen – Love—will liberate you from your past so you can align with the Divine, feel empowered and fulfilled, and dive into the life for which you came here.

Allow what you resist and liberate this new energy to be present with yourself in a new way.

Listen deeply to what you previously ignored. What is your being trying to tell you, now that you have this liberated energy at your disposal?

Love and learn from what you hear. Now you can act from the wisdom in your being to move through life with joy, love and inspiration, allowing your experience versus resisting it, and listening to your heart, your core values and your body's wisdom versus ignoring them. Now, you are loving and accepting what you learn about yourself versus criticizing, doubting, and judging it.

This leads to:

*Realizing the real you
*Confidence and trusting yourself at the core
*Living undivided and in oneness with yourself and not at odds
*Opening up to a life of fulfilment and joy.

For more information visit: http://www.divinefemi-nineflow.com/PDF/Five_Steps_to_Dive_into_the_Divine_Feminine_Flow.pdf

The Sedona Method

Originally developed by Lester Levenson, the Sedona Method is now being taught by his successor, Hale Dwoskin who leads workshops and retreats in Sedona, AZ and other locations.

If you review your life, you will probably recall many instances that you have let go. We generally let go either by accident or when our backs are against the wall, and we have no other choice.

As you focus on reawakening and strengthening this natural ability within yourself by practicing the Sedona Method, you will be able to bring releasing under your conscious control, making it a viable option throughout your everyday life.

There are five ways to approach the process of releasing, all leading to the same result: liberating your natural ability to let go of any unwanted emotion on the spot, allowing some of the suppressed energy in your subconscious to dissipate.

The first way is by choosing to let go of the unwanted feeling.

The second way is to welcome the feeling—allowing the emotion just to be.

The third way is to dive into the core of the emotion.

The fourth way is by holistically embracing both sides of any issue or belief.

And the last way of releasing—the fifth way—helps you to discover the beingness that you already are here and now.

These are the five basic releasing questions serving as the foundation of The Sedona Method:

What is your *now* feeling?

Could you welcome/allow that feeling?

Could you let it go?

Would you let it go?

When?

Learn more at www.sedona.com

Heartspeak

As the human race grows in awareness, the interventions of yesterday become inadequate. At the cutting edge of mind-body medicine, HeartSpeak is the next-generation healing tool you have been waiting for.

Feelings are the primary drivers of thoughts, actions, behaviours, and bodily functions. With HeartSpeak, you are more capable of *responding* – rather than reacting.

With HeartSpeak, you can regain *conscious choice* once more.

During a HeartSpeak session, you will be gently and purposefully guided through challenging emotions, and will come out the other side with your triggers softened and with more ease in your life. You will be amazed at how easy it is. *And you will love it!*

Why HeartSpeak?

As the human race grows in awareness, the interventions of yesterday become inadequate. At the cutting edge of mind-body medicine, HeartSpeak is the next-generation healing tool you have been waiting for.

Feelings are the primary drivers of thoughts, actions, behaviours, and bodily functions. With HeartSpeak, you are more capable of *responding* – rather than reacting. With HeartSpeak, you can regain conscious *choice* once more.

HeartSpeak principles are based on cutting-edge research from the fields of neuroscience, the science of feeling (i.e. affective science), and the science of learning and memory. During a HeartSpeak session, you will be gently and purposefully guided through challenging emotions that trigger unwanted reactions.

Once you are through the challenging emotion, you will pivot to a more preferable, pleasant feeling. After the HeartSpeak clearing, you experience an immediate sense of relief, and next you will notice that triggers are softened and there's more ease in your life.

You will love it!

HeartSpeak can be used on any feeling that may be distributing your ease. For example, HeartSpeak can be used to reduce certain physical symptoms, such as chronic pain, muscle tension and fatigue.

HeartSpeak can also be used to lessen the emotionality of feeling symptoms, such as painful memories, and of anxiousness, glumness, and stress. There are so many applications for HeartSpeak. If you can feel it, you can clear it!

To benefit from HeartSpeak, visit a HeartSpeak practitioner, or take a course and learn the HeartSpeak Principles, so that you will have the tools to help yourself.

Courses are offered in various formats: in-person, online live and online video – choose the format that works best for you.

Thousands have been helped through HeartSpeak all over the world.

Are you ready for it?

www.heartspeak.com

Theta Healing

One of the most powerful energy-healing techniques, ThetaHealing® is a process of meditation that we believe creates physical, psychological, and spiritual healing using the Theta brain wave. While in a pure Theta state of mind, we are able to connect to the Creator of All That Is through focused prayer.

It is through the Creator of All That Is that we learned how to create physical healing, progress spiritually, and find a path to enlightenment.

We all have different motivation for learning something like ThetaHealing®. Some people are searching for knowledge, some are merely curious, and others have less altruistic motives. But the majority of people who learn it are pure of heart and seeking to expand abilities lying dormant in their minds. This is what ThetaHealing® is designed to do, teaching people to harness their psychic abilities through spiritual awareness. (Theta Healing.com)

Made in the USA
Columbia, SC
13 October 2021